C0-CZW-464

Private Readings/
Public Texts

Private Readings/ Public Texts

Playreaders' Constructs of Theatre Audiences

Kenneth Krauss

Rutherford ● Madison ● Teaneck
Fairleigh Dickinson University Press
London and Toronto: Associated University Presses

© 1993 by Kenneth Krauss

All rights reserved. Authorization to photocopy items for internal or personal use, or the internal or personal use of specific clients, is granted by the copyright owner, provided that a base fee of $10.00, plus eight cents per page, per copy is paid directly to the Copyright Clearance Center, 27 Congress Street, Salem, Massachusetts 01970. [0-8386-3496-6/93 $10.00 + 8¢ pp, pc.]

Associated University Presses
440 Forsgate Drive
Cranbury, NJ 08512

Associated University Presses
25 Sicilian Avenue
London WC1A 2QH, England

Associated University Presses
P.O. Box 338, Port Credit
Mississauga, Ontario
L5G 4L8 Canada

The paper used in this publication meets the requirements
of the American National Standard for Permanence of Paper
for Printed Library Materials Z39.48-1984.

Library of Congress Cataloging-in-Publication Data

Krauss, Kenneth, 1948–
    Private readings/public texts : playreaders' constructs of theatre
audiences / Kenneth Krauss.
        p. cm.
    Includes bibliographical references and index.
    ISBN 0-8386-3496-6 (alk. paper)
    1. Drama—Explication. 2. Reader-response criticism. 3. Theater
audiences. I. Title.
PN1707.K73   1993
801'.952—dc20   91-58945
                                                                    CIP

PRINTED IN THE UNITED STATES OF AMERICA

PN
1707
K73
1993

To My Father
and
To the Memory of My Mother:

πῶς οὖν τις αὐτὰ διαλαβὼν ὀρθῶς κρινεῖ;
—Eur., *El.*, 373

And to Laszlo:

A kicsi fekete kutya jó van . . .

Contents

Acknowledgments

Many people helped me as I struggled through this project. Robert Bone encouraged and critiqued my approach to reading playscripts and my analysis of the writings of those who have previously written on the topic. Martin Meisel carefully read and offered lucid criticism of the changing and developing drafts. Maxine Greene questioned, quite probingly, a number of my theoretical points. Lucy Calkins provided a thought-provoking challenge regarding how the study related to pedagogy and learning. Howard Stein anticipated and noted possible contradictions in my readings of Aristotle.

I especially wish to thank three friends, former teaching colleagues, whose interest in some of the issues raised by my study assisted enormously in the otherwise lonesome enterprise of writing a book: Edward Davenport, Nancy Hazelton, and Barbara Shollar.

I also wish to thank my colleagues in the Department of English at the College of Saint Rose in Albany, New York, for their great validation in this endeavor and to express my appreciation to the College of Saint Rose for the Mini grant which helped support me during my final revisions of the manuscript. I would especially like to thank Catherine Cavanaugh for her great help in reading the manuscript and proofs.

Private Readings/
Public Texts

1
Introduction

While inventing a biography for William Shakespeare, Jorge Luis Borges characterizes the actor as someone "who on stage plays at being another before a gathering of people who play at taking him for that other person."[1] This definition of performer *and* audience as "players" is crucial to an understanding not only of theatre but of drama.

Many of us get to know plays from the page rather than from the stage. Because we are taught to read playscripts as we read other forms of literature—not regarding them as the bases of performances but as texts for silent study and subsequent discussion—we tend to forget that such scripts are intended to be played by both actor and audience. We as readers may allow the actor to enter our consciousnesses as the player, but the audience, "who play at taking [the actor] for that other person," we may disregard or devalue. Indeed, if what has been written on reading drama accurately reflects how we read playscripts, most readers spend little time and energy on the audience's role in a play.

The debate on whether drama ought to be studied through reading playscripts or through theatregoing has gone on, at least in the English-speaking world, since the first half of the seventeenth century. Around 1634 Sir Richard Baker declared that "a play *read,* hath not half the pleasure of a Play *Acted:* for though it have the pleasure of *ingenious Speeches,* yet it wants the pleasure of *Gracefull action:* and we may well acknowledg, that *Gracefulness* of *action,* is the greatest pleasure of a play. . . ."[2] Around the same time, Lucius Cary, Lord Falkland, wrote to request a copy of a playbook, noting of the play, "[I]f I valued it so high at the single hearing, when myne eares could not catch half the wordes, what must I do now in the reading when I may pause upon it?"[3]

In spite of the obvious advantages of seeing plays over reading them, in the late twentieth century even the most adamant proponent of theatregoing cannot entirely dismiss the importance of reading playscripts or, as I call it throughout this study, *playread-*

ing.[4] In our own time there are too many plays and far too few opportunities to see them. Theatre tickets are often expensive, and actually going to a play, for those accustomed to staying at home with radio, television, and video tape players, may prove extremely inconvenient or even impossible. Moreover, unlike those who lived four or even two centuries before us, we who are today engaged in reading, studying, and enjoying literature accept playscripts as examples of a legitimate literary genre.

Still, there are several ways by which readers may approach the written text of a play: they may, for example, trace the plot and try to create in their minds a strand of fictive narrative, which is never explicit in playscripts; or they may carefully examine the language of the script's speeches. They in fact frequently do both whenever they read a playscript or, more importantly, whenever they read any piece of literature.

Nonetheless, however they go about playreading, readers must be prepared also to read playscripts differently from the way they read other literary works, if only because playscripts follow a distinctive format. Yet the conventions of the playscript—the use of descriptive directions and dialogue—are in themselves made necessary by the requirements of performance. Playscripts, then, need to be thought of and thus approached as bound for the stage. Still, because they are written and because it is usually easier for us to read playscripts than to see and hear plays, readers, especially those engaged in the study of literature, find themselves struggling to make literary sense of what must always remain, at least on some level, some set of instructions for performers— more a blueprint for a work of theatre art than a work of literature complete in itself.

A number of writers concerned with playreading, notably Roger Gross (discussed in chapter 2) and Kirsten Nigro (discussed in chapter 3), define the playscript as "a symbolic notation."[5] This definition, when coupled with a suggestion made by Thelma Altschuler and Richard Paul Janow that "[a] play in print is to a play on stage as the orchestral score is to the performed symphony,"[6] leads us to an especially useful analogy. We may compare the reader of the musical score, who through sight-reading creates the music in imagination, to the playreader, who through reading the playscript imaginatively creates the play. Perhaps the vital part in this comparison lies in the fact that the sight reader can imagine that the music "implied" by the score is being *heard;* this sight reader, then, not only actively *produces* and *listens* to the music, but can imagine the auditors' responses and can evaluate or criticize the musical experience. Hence the highly trained reader retains an identity separate from both orchestra and audience. For play-readers, the implications of this process are particularly significant.[7]

In addition to readers' problems which arise from the format of the playscript and from the need of the playscript to be staged, difficulties emerge from the discrepancies between reading a playscript and watching a production of a play. What we are used to doing today while reading literature is typically private and personal; yet what we do, as we sit in an auditorium, is inevitably public and communal. Early in *Shakespearean Negotiations,* Stephen Greenblatt makes this crucial differentiation between the audience for fiction and the audience for drama:

> [T]he theater manifestly addresses its audience as a collectivity. The model is not, as with the nineteenth-century novel, the individual reader who withdraws from the public world of affairs to the privacy of the hearth but the crowd that gathers together in a public play space.[8]

If we accept that playscripts are destined for production, our readings ought to take into account the theatrical response to the performed dramatic text. This statement does not mean to suggest that while reading a playscript we should pay more attention to our imagined production than to the text itself or that, as Harry Berger unfairly summarizes the approach of stage-oriented critics such as Styan, playreading "is irresponsible unless it imitates playgoing."[9]

What Michael Issacharoff and Robin Jones refer to as the "text/performance dichotomy"[10] has led some to the fallacious notion that the reader must either follow a literary or a theatrical approach while reading a play; the notion, notes Austin E. Quigley, especially with reference to modern drama, "is not easily maintained in the face of so widespread a concern among dramatists of so many kinds for linking reform in the structure of drama with reform in the structure of the performance environment."[11] If we are able to keep in mind, while reading a particular playscript, the "story" revealed by the play, the meanings of what is spoken by the play's characters, and the way(s) the play looks and sounds in performance, we can nonetheless begin to value what audiences do during the course of a play.

This study contends that playscripts are best read when readers are able to construct a sense of the responses of the theatre audience. This contention, that readers ought to have a clear sense of the play's theatre audience(s) while they read playscripts, may not sound very innovative. After all, we are taught that literary criticism began more than two millennia ago with a treatise that mentioned prominently the relationship between tragedy—specifically the dramatic text of tragedy—and its spectators.[12] It is precisely because our drama criticism traces itself back to Aristotle's *Poetics* that many believe that the process of reading dramatic texts has been more than sufficiently explored in the existing theoretical and critical literature. In reality, however, much has been written on the plays we read but very little on our reading of plays.

An audience-oriented approach to playreading must be careful not to discount the value of reading a playscript just to find out what happens. Nor should it disparage the worth of attentive scrutiny of a play's dialogue. In effect, both of these activities, the former drawn from reading fiction, the latter from reading poetry, are vital components of the larger process in which the reader conceptualizes the dramatic text on stage; indeed, this process, given the nature of dramatic literature, is imperative to an understanding of the playscript as a written text of a performance on stage. Nonetheless, as important as it is for playreaders to be able to comprehend a dramatic text in light of its actual or potential productions, the very nature of the theatre experience, which transpires between those working on stage and those watching and listening in the house, is made accessible to readers only when they look at a playscript with an awareness of the requisite presence of the audience.

Although in the preceding paragraph I describe (much as Borges does) communication in the theatre as occurring between those connected with the performance and those seated in the auditorium, I do not mean to imply that what happens on stage dictates what the audience does. Of course, as Marvin Carlson observes, "much theatre theory still regards the theatre performance as something created and set before an essentially passive audience,"[13] but spectators continue to have minds of their own. The ultimate fate of most productions depends less on the reviews of drama critics than on what the audience makes of the play. Communication in the theatre necessarily goes back and forth: between those on stage and the audience *and* between the audience and those on stage. For artistic as well as financial reasons, a play does not, *cannot* run when the house is empty. Drama requires an audience—a point made with extraordinary eloquence by the leader of the traveling theatrical troupe in *Hamlet* (or rather by his reincarnation in Tom Stoppard's *Rosencrantz and Guildenstern Are Dead*). In recalling how the tragedians discovered in the midst of performance that their audience of two spectators had fled, the Player complains,

> We pledged our identities, secure in the conventions of our trade, that someone would be watching. And then, gradually, no one was. . . . Even then, habit and a stubborn trust that our audience spied upon us from behind the nearest bush, forced our bodies to blunder on long after they had emptied of meaning, until like runaway carts they dragged to a halt. No one came forward. No one shouted at us. The silence was unbearable, it imposed itself upon us; it was obscene.[14]

Before an empty house, what "happens" on stage ceases to be drama. Thus, playreaders who struggle to imagine the dramatic text in light of the theatre text must decide whether they are actually thinking about a *performance* of a play, which takes place before an audience, or merely about a *rehearsal*.

To talk of the playreader's audience, however, is not quite as simple as I may have made it sound. As Alfred Harbage, trying to hypothesize just who watched the plays at the Globe, laments, "Audiences leave few traces behind, few means of vindication. Plays leave their texts behind for the ages to judge."[15] We possess a number of scripts of plays from ancient Athens and from Elizabethan England, but we have remarkably little on the audiences who saw those scripts performed. Even with modern theatre audiences, about whom we can and occasionally do know much, it is still difficult to apply to our reading of playscripts what we can discover about their responses, because playreading for us has, for the most part, relied heavily on plot-oriented, language-oriented, and stage-oriented readings. Thus, having asserted that playreaders need to read with a sense of audience response, I have placed myself in a position in which I am compelled to address a number of related problems.

This study advocates audience-oriented playreading and holds fast to the notion that without this kind of playreading, readers of playscripts are not just severely handicapped but doomed never to encounter the plays in playscripts. Even though what we have learned about reading from our own readings of novels and poems may be productively applied to our playreading and even if we concentrate on what the playscript appears to say about what is happening on stage, we must be able, while reading a playscript, to construct (and in some instances, to reconstruct) that transaction between audience and play.

As I mentioned earlier, the usual model of how theatre works defines the play as active and the audience as passive. The traditional literature on playreading (reviewed in chapter 2), like the body of traditional dramatic theory, has been, as Susan Bennett asserts in her study of the theatre audience's role, "concerned with aesthetic formalism, rather than the spectators' demands and expectations, as a shaping element of both playscript and performance practice."[16] This theoretical inclination reflects, to an extent, the attitudes of some of those who are more practically involved in the theatre. Yet, as Herbert Blau confides, in his study of the audience, when an actor boasts "I had the audience in the palm of my hand," his or her remark constitutes "a claim of power verging on delusion."[17] At any rate, traditional dramatic theory tends to regard what happens on stage as acting upon the spectators. Hence, playwrights are often said to shape the audience's experience and directors are defined as the interpreters of the script for those in the house; theatregoers (and playreaders too) are urged to take in the dramatic text in the proper way, which is often the way that the playwright or director or performers have presented it, or at least intended to present it. To an important degree, of course, this model is accurate, for audiences do respond to what is mounted before them.

Still, in this context *respond* clearly proves to be a deceptive word; although it is commonly used to denote our experience of a work of art, as with listeners responding to a symphony or viewers to a painting, it also connotes the very reactive processes implied in the model described above, in which the audience is assigned the role of compliant receivers and the transaction between stage and house is broadly depicted as one-way, from the former to the latter.[18]

Yet it should be obvious to anyone who has ever gone to the theatre that things are rarely so unilateral. Spectators are sometimes all-too-active in their responses, weeping, moaning, laughing, shouting, throwing things, even getting up to leave before the final curtain. Moreover, in the auditorium, watching and hearing a play are rarely passive activities: to varying degrees, engaged audience members are busy observing set details, listening to dialogue, attending to the gestures and actions of the performers— in short, involved in apprehending what they construe is in front of them *and* around them. Most importantly, the audience, both individually and collectively, attempts to comprehend the experience.

Those on stage strive to present the play to the audience, and the audience struggles to make sense of what is being presented. This two-way transaction may be difficult to detect readily with respect to established professional productions. A hit on Broadway may run for years to the delight of its seemingly compliant audiences. Nonetheless, before its New York opening the play inevitably went through out-of-town tryouts and in-town previews during which the director carefully and deliberately studied house response. During this phase of production, when the show may still be adjusted and altered, what audiences make of the performances is all-important because it can provide the soundest test of whether or not the audience does what the director in fact hopes they will do with (and perhaps to) the play. Even after the play opens and the show is set, audience response is never static, never completely consistent. And if the hit that has run for years does begin to fade and sag and thereby tire audiences, its producers either bring in someone to sharpen and polish it or allow the show to close.

In the traditional model, the play—the script and its production—conveys meaning to the audience. In real life, however, the audience experiences what happens on stage and tries to make something of it. In other words, the play not only occurs on stage but also in the auditorium, and meaning is determined not only by the performance of the script but also by what the audience does with the performance.

An important part of the play is, therefore, necessarily largely absent from the playscript itself. We may believe that we can detect traces of the audience in the written texts of plays, more in some playscripts than in others. Yet, for the most part, the requisite role played by the theatre audience is virtually unlocatable on the page. It thus becomes imperative that playreaders regard the dramatic text in its playscript form as a literary work which requires them not only to attend to action and language and to consider the visible and audible elements that would emerge on stage during a performance of the play, *but also* to construct a sense of audience(s) while they are reading.

An obvious question, then, is just who *is* this audience that the playreader is supposed to imagine? Is this audience merely that vague one rhetorically implied by the script? Is it a hypothetical one based on sociological or historical information? Is it a reconstruction, based on hard data, about *actual* spectators who came to a specific performance? Or is it a speculation about an audience who never got the chance to see the play or who actually did see it, but under circumstances that differed radically from the actual production that was staged?

This study maintains that the playreader's audience can and should be all of these, that each of these four possible "audiences" offers a viable way of reading the play implied by the playscript. Above all, this study asserts that the playreader must keep in mind that audiences are comprised of human beings who, as human beings, are to some degree necessarily the products of their specific circumstances—cultural, political, economic, theatrical, and so on.

The second and third chapters of this book survey the two bodies of modern critical literature which are relevant to the general topic of playreading and which consequently bear heavily upon the issue of playreaders' ideas about theatre audiences. The material that I review in chapter 2 I call "playreading literature"; it is comprised of an assortment of books and dissertations, all theoretically object-oriented in their attempts to discuss how we read plays. For the most part, and perhaps understandably in light of their critical perspectives, the best of these studies focus on the language of the playscript, on the design of the plot, and on how the dramatic text in the playscript has been and may be embodied on stage. However, the very critical perspectives which enable this literature such insight in these areas also render it virtually blind in regard to the audience and the playreader. This literature, though inventive and often insightful, has been relatively difficult to collect, mostly because the writers of this literature say little about each other or about playreading as a field.

The material that I review in chapter 3 relates to what has become known as reader-response criticism.[19] As critics all too readily concede, the term "reader-response," unlike the German *Rezeption*, is a loose one. Nevertheless, unlike the writers of the "playreading literature" discussed in chapter 2, those whom we call reader-response critics are more conscious that they are participating in an ongoing dialogue and are more scrupulous in relating to the work of their colleagues. Unfortunately, as Nigro, in an unusually perceptive article on reading Latin American plays, remarks,

> most practitioners of reader-response criticism have turned to narrative and poetry in order to explore the ramifications of this premise

[that the dynamic relationship established between text and reader is what produces meaning], with scant attention being given to drama.[20]

The writings of reader-response critics, enable us to consider what a reader does while reading a play, whether envisioning the set, imagining sound effects, or constructing the theatre audience; but ironically, there is virtually nothing on playreading. The reasons for this neglect by reader-response critics are only in part theoretical; other causes reside in the institution of literary criticism.

Both bodies of critical literature are for the most part in English. My review begins, in chapter 2, with the rise of the New Criticism as a potent force in British and North American education after the Second World War; it then traces subsequent developments (such as structuralism) that have influenced Anglo-American literary theory. My review proceeds, in chapter 3, by examining reader-response criticism, again largely a North American and almost exclusively Anglophone movement, thanks to widely-distributed translations and to European writers (such as Wolfgang Iser) who write in English as well as in their native languages.

There is of course an important European tradition, initiated by the German Romantics, on the reading of dramatic texts. As Marvin Carlson reminds us, Schlegel maintained that "[a] play upon which much art has been lavished but which lacks the art of pleasing belongs in the study and not on the stage."[21] Goethe believed Shakespeare's poetic vision was too expansive and complicated for the stage and, as Carlson puts it, "suited only to a theatre of the mind."[22] More recently, French critic Anne Ubersfeld, in *Lire le théâtre* (1977) and *L'école du spectateur* (1982), has offered an intriguing semiological analysis of how the dramatic text communicates with the reader.[23] I discuss Ubersfeld and semiological studies of drama in my third chapter. Yet the real focus of interest for European writers continues to be the dramatic text-object, rather than what transpires between reader and text. Schlegel and Goethe initiated this trend by scrutinizing the script, which they argued may or may not be at its best when read in private. Ubersfeld and others, in spite of (and also because of) their intense interest in communications between text and reader (in that order), ultimately make the text (dramatic or theatre), if not the only active party, at least the preeminent one of the two.

In chapter 4, following these surveys, I draw from the literature four specific constructs for playreader audiences. These include the rhetorical audience, the hypothetical audience, the actual audience, and the speculated audience. In chapter 5 I illustrate these through spectator-oriented readings of a modern playscript, *Les bonnes* by Jean Genet. I offer, first, possible conventional readings that are not audience-oriented; I then give four separate but related readings, each one emphasizing a specific audience construct which readers may deploy.

Before going any further, however, I need to define that essential character whom I have so frequently mentioned: the *reader*, also known here as the *playreader*. The reader whom I have in mind is neither the theatre specialist for whom Richard Hornby and David Grote write, nor the very general reader toward whom Ronald Hayman directs his efforts. I am interested in the armchair theatregoer who is in some way a member of an academic community and is engaged in the study of drama largely (though not exclusively) through playreading; this includes advanced secondary students and also undergraduate and graduate students, as well as these students' teachers.

Thus, my reader to some degree coincides with that of Cleanth Brooks and Robert Heilman and of the many playreading handbook writers of the 1960s. To the extent that Kenneth Thorpe Rowe's reader may be a student of literature, my reader resembles his. To the extent that Gross's reader is in some way connected to an academic institution and Nigro's North American scholar is reading to teach, my reader overlaps with theirs.

My reader's motivation for reading stems from an involvement with and commitment to learning about the literature of the theatre through the reading of playscripts. Moreover, my reader goes on to discuss the playscript and the play or to write about them. Thus, my reader must be able to refer not merely to his or her private reading, but to that public text which is generated by the interaction of Borges's key *players* in the theatre, the audience and the production.[24]

2
The Literature of Playreading

Introduction

This chapter, in surveying the literature which over the last forty-five years has explicitly discussed the reading of dramatic texts, attempts to show how this literature slowly became aware of the concept of a playreader's theatre audience. Whether or not there in fact exists a corpus of work on playreading is certainly debatable. I believe that there indeed is a collection of books through which we can follow the fragmented and dislocated development of playreading theory, or, if not of theory, then at least of the evolution of an oft-interrupted dialogue on playreading, the implications of which arise from theoretical formulations.

The books that comprise this literature are drawn from diverse contexts; they range from textbooks intended for classroom use to critical and theoretical studies. They include guides for the general reader, doctoral dissertations, and even self-help manuals designed to assist secondary students in writing essays on drama. However, they all share the premises that reading playscripts differs from reading other kinds of literature and that this difference presents a problem which, in order to read playscripts, readers must solve.

In identifying a body of playreading literature, this chapter distinguishes between studies that consciously scrutinize how we read playscripts and those that focus on other aspects of drama or theatre. For example, a number of books, like Alan B. Howes's *Teaching Literature to Adolescents: Plays* and Joseph Mersand's *Teaching the Drama in Secondary Schools,* look at the problem of teaching playscripts. Others, like Bernard Beckerman's *Dynamics of Drama,* examine the nature of dramatic literature or, like Peter Brook's *The Empty Space,* discuss the nature of a play's staged performance. In all of these there is, often by necessity, an implicit working definition of playreading. Yet it is in full-length treatments devoted to an explication of the reading of playscripts, in which writers are compelled to develop and state more fully and explicitly their positions on the topic, that we may discern what the definitions only briefly suggested elsewhere in the critical discourse genuinely entail.

An important example of a book which does not primarily concern itself with playreading but which borders on the topic is J. L. Styan's *Elements of Drama* (1960). Styan is a critic whom many writers on playreading highly recommend (especially for this book, rather than for *The Dramatic Experience: A Guide to the Reading of Plays,* discussed later in this chapter). What *Elements of Drama* discusses is "what to look for and how to look for it, both in the theatre and in the text of the play."[1] Styan believes that "an understanding of the processes of the theatrical experience is necessary for the full appreciation of the play";[2] this locates him among performance- or stage-oriented critics. Nevertheless, although in this book Styan frequently mentions reading plays, he does not provide—nor, given his topic, should he perhaps be expected to—an expansive, a completely coherent explanation of the process, nor does he feel obliged to argue his view of playreading. Thus, in this work by Styan and in the works of other drama and theatre critics of enormous insight, there emerge the shadowy outlines of a discussion of playreading upon which are built discussions of other matters.

A more recent, and perhaps more visible, instance of establishing such a foundation occurs in Anthony Manna's dissertation on stage-centered teaching methods (1976). In describing his work with secondary school English teachers, Manna states in his introduction that his answer to the question, "*How* does a play mean? . . . derives from an assumption about how a playwright structures the incidents, creates the characters, and uses the language which convey the play's meaning to an individual reader."[3] Manna's statement alerts us to a widespread trend: writers on drama almost always assume that we read plays in a certain manner, and the manner to which Manna refers, in which the *dramatist's* structuring of the text takes precedence over all other factors in the playreading process, is the one most critics share. Perhaps the reason he and they fail to offer a more detailed explanation or justification comes from their own assumption that this view of playreading is so obvious that readers do not need to have it explained or justified. Unfortunately, the assumption rests upon theories about literature, drama, and theatre which not only promote this view but which tend to disable views that differ from or oppose it.

With this in mind, let us turn to the various works that make up the literature on reading plays. As noted in chapter 1, the books contained in this body of literature are all in English. They first appeared at the end of World War II, when returning servicemen, encouraged by the GI Bill, flooded American colleges, and textbook publishers strove to supply new approaches to entering freshmen. Over the next four-and-a-half decades, as more and more readers both in and out of school picked up playscripts, a succession of authors offered them assistance. Gradually, almost imperceptibly, there developed a sense that for the reader of playscripts the audience could not be entirely ignored.

Two New Critics Direct Our Reading

Any review of the literature of playreading must begin with *Understanding Drama* by Cleanth Brooks and Robert B. Heilman, published in 1945.[4] The book has come to be regarded as the New Criticism's position paper on reading playscripts. Of course, making any one book representative of the New Critical movement is rather unfair, for as Frank Lentricchia reminds us, "[T]he New Criticism was in fact no monolith but an inconsistent and sometimes confused movement; the differences between variously identified New Critics . . . are real."[5] Nonetheless, there are a number of common traits that run through the work of those whom we today know as New Critics—traits that may indeed be found in *Understanding Drama*: a preoccupation with close reading and with language, a turn away from all outside the specific literary text under scrutiny, and the objectification of the literary text, which, as Terry Eagleton notes, was made distinct "from both author and reader."[6]

That *Understanding Drama* was the only book by New Critics to look at the reading of drama made it especially susceptible to attacks by later writers. Roger Gross dismisses this "very influential book,"[7] noting that the authors' "description of the theatrical medium . . . is a series of prejudices disguised as observations."[8] He further denounces their criteria as "contrived in too great isolation from the world's dramatic repertory" to include some of the indisputably great works of dramatic literature.[9] Richard Hornby says the book "must now be considered a failure" because its authors were unduly influenced by "the theatre practices of their day, which . . . were those of naturalism."[10] Marvin Carlson, a more neutral commentator, synopsizes that

> After a general introduction to the drama as a literary form, a series
> of plays—"arranged in a scale of ascending difficulty" from *Everyman*
> to *The Way of the World*—was analyzed according to the principles of
> this school [New Criticism], in terms of characterization, structure,
> theme, symbol, and Brooks's central critical concerns: unity, balance,
> metaphor, and irony. . . . As a genre, Brooks and Heilman consider
> drama closer to poetry than to prose fiction, since these two forms
> share a high concentration of effect in language, and both are strictly
> controlled by the restrictions of the form.[11]

This capsule view, faithful though it may be to the book's contents,
implies through its use of the passive voice and of a rather dead-
pan tone what may be Carlson's underlying skepticism.

Although many recent critics have disparaged and even dis-
missed the New Critics, we may now be able to evaluate the
strengths and weaknesses of *Understanding Drama* without con-
demning it. It is a unique book on reading playscripts, both for
the way which it tries to lead the reader through specific works
of dramatic literature and for its stubborn refusal to consider the
play as anything other than a literary text.

Understanding Drama was written for classroom use. Henry Holt
and Company (in a promotional chit pasted onto the back of the
front cover of my copy) promised "a new kind of text-anthology
suitable for the freshman, sophomore survey, or brief drama
course," which "analyzes each play and emphasizes the character-
istics, development, and special problems of the drama." In the
prefatory "Letter to Teachers and Students," Brooks and Heilman explain that this is "primarily a manual for reading drama,
with the essentially modest aim that such a term connotes, though
also with all the importance . . . that the richest and fullest definition of *reading* must imply."[12] The authors—or "editors" as they
call themselves—deny that their commentaries are meant to be
"prescriptive": "They offer *a* reading of the play, but this does
not purport to be *the* reading." The editors also contradict the
implication that they wish to discard drama's history.[13]

This hybrid "anthology-text" of dramas was unique in its time.
Unlike the collections of playscripts before it, *Understanding Drama*
provides an ongoing and consistent commentary before and after
the playscripts it contains and even between each act. Its arrange-
ment of material differs radically from that of contemporary anthologies (to which the editors refer us for scripts discussed but
not included),[14] for its order is not chronological (as in *Treasury
of the Theatre*, ed. Burns Mantle and John Gassner, 1935), nor
determined by geography or period (as in *Modern Continental*

Plays, ed. S. M. Tucker, 1929), nor generic (as in *Types of World Tragedy,* ed. Robert M. Smith, 1928). Rather, it is clearly a *critical* anthology. By surrounding the included plays with critical commentary and with questions that have theoretical implications, and by placing this sort of material between each act, the editors try to direct and shape our readings of the eight playscripts contained in the book (and of the fifteen discussed at the end). And although the theory behind their discussion may seem at times unsuited to an appreciation of playscripts, their guided tour through playreading is, as a method to lead us from cover to cover, brilliant.

Reading for Brooks and Heilman means maintaining a sharp focus on the text itself, subjecting it to a microscopic formalist view, as opposed to the macroscopic historical view they claim to accept. The editors may state that they do not "intend to discount the claims of literary history," but they do take it for granted that "much of the historical material, of course, will be provided by the teacher . . ." Meanwhile, they concede, "Teachers who wish to stress the historical approach will find a succinct history of the drama in Appendix B."[15] Some may feel that their four-and-a-half page appendix on two-and-a-half millennia of theatre[16] is not so much succinct as it is unduly condensed, and that this "manual" would be truer to itself without it. Moreover, this overview of theatre history cannot hide a crucial flaw in the editors' approach to the study of dramatic literature—that is, without the historical-theatrical context to supply the concrete circumstances of production, the reader has very few resources for comprehending the playscript as anything other than a linguistic work.

So, *playreading* for Brooks and Heilman really means scrutinizing the dramatic text, especially the language of the dialogue of the dramatic text, outside a theatrical context. This kind of reading diminishes the value of the theatrical text. Such a diminution is immediately evident, for example, in the editors' characterization of the "*pantomime*—a very old art . . . which, deprived as it is of the use of words, can get at the inner life of its characters only very indirectly."[17] This remark is an early indication that language, "our richest and most subtle means of significant expression,"[18] is the editors' major, if not only, ingredient of dramatic art. After extended comparisons with other genres, they admit that poetry and fiction have "greater resources" but argue that "[i]n proper hands, drama can make its own way very effectively."[19]

As if to remove all doubt about what they believe the playscript to be, they conclude that "a literary form which wholly depends upon dialogue obviously faces complex difficulties."[20] With such logic, Brooks and Heilman depreciate the significance of those parts of the playscript (and thus, of the play) that are not in the dialogue, such as stage directions and set and character descriptions. Hence, their entr'acte comments, questions, and assignments require only an examination of the play's speeches. The implication, in spite of their protests to the contrary, is that drama, in its linguistic and literary purity, is best appreciated not on the stage but on the page.

At first glance, the editors' attitude toward the stage may appear consistent with Aristotle's remark in the *Poetics* regarding the unimportance of the spectacle *(opsis)* of tragedy or, as Gerald Else maintains "the visual aspect of the dramatic characters":[21]

> Spectacle, while highly effective, is quite foreign to the art and has nothing to do with poetry. Indeed the effect of tragedy does not depend on its performance by actors, and, moreover, for achieving the spectacular effects the art of the costumier is more authoritative than that of the poet.[22]

However, their own summary of the *Poetics*[23] (quoted below) makes little of Aristotle's statement, "Tragedy must not depend upon spectacle . . ." Nor do the editors appear to have drawn their partiality for the dramatic over the theatrical text from more recent writers, such as Brander Matthews, whom they know as an anthologist;[24] at least, they never refer to him in a critical vein. Their lack of references, of course, is characteristic of the New Criticism, which in concentrating on the text deliberately tends to avoid addressing the related critical discourse—again, because for the editors (and presumably for the undergraduate reader) the text alone is of importance. Thus, guided by a literary theory which holds that only the words on the page are genuinely meaningful, Brooks and Heilman owe their position on the primacy of the dramatic text to the New Criticism rather than to any allegiance to Aristotle or any other drama or theatre tradition.

Because New Critics so rarely look to other commentators, it may be informative to see what use the editors make of Aristotle, whom they feel obliged not to ignore. Their reading of the *Poetics* (as translated by S. N. Butcher, whose rendering of Aristotle they enclose in quotes) reduces it to nineteen points and emphasizes ideas on form, such as the depiction of time on stage, the structure of incidents in the plot, and the nature of character. Those parts of the treatise that pertain to the audience's responses are con-

densed and worded in a manner that diminishes or eliminates
their interactive quality:

> 3. ". . . through pity and fear" it [tragedy] effects "the proper pur-
> gation of these emotions." . . .
> 10. The effect of pity and terror "is best produced when the events
> come on us by surprise; and the effect is heightened when, at the
> same time, they follow as cause and effect."
> 11. An aid to the proper effect of tragedy is the reversal, "by which
> the action veers round to its opposite, subject always to our rule of
> probability or necessity" (this is really a definition of *dramatic irony*).
> 12. The proper effect is not produced by "the spectacle of the
> virtuous man brought from prosperity to adversity." . . .
> 14. Tragedy must not depend upon spectacle, upon extraneous
> aids, or upon the "monstrous," "for we must not demand of Tragedy
> any and every pleasure, but only that which is proper to it."[25]

The editors turn Aristotle's spotlight away from the dynamic interplay between audience and play and onto the play itself. Audience feelings are converted into dramatic "effects." Seen from
this point of view, the *Poetics* becomes nothing but a discussion of
the dramatic literary object.

Throughout the literature of playreading, what writers make
of the *Poetics* frequently says more about their ideas than about
those of the ancient philosopher. For the time being, it is enough
to observe from the editors' digest of Aristotle (albeit Butcher's
Aristotle) that their orientation leans heavily toward a formalism
which discounts the value of *response,* specifically of the responses
of audience to the play and by extension, of the responses of the
reader to the playscript. Thus, as a guide to the process of reading
plays their book is self-contradictory: it ostensibly encourages the
reader to read plays but does not, or perhaps more accurately
cannot, offer any sustained discourse on the process in which the
reader is engaged.

Roger Gross is justified in calling *Understanding Drama* "a very
influential book" because as a critical anthology of dramatic literature it both served as a model for college drama textbooks that
would follow and set the tone for drama courses developed over
the next thirty years. In addition, it represented to many the New
Criticism's "official line" on drama; its methods of reading are
indeed representative of and consistent with those of American
New Critics, and as such the book (in conjunction with other New
Critical works) led several generations of American students to-

ward a more careful consideration of the language of the playscript, if only the language of the dialogue.

It is important to add, of course, that several British writers
who may be identified as New Critics, such as G. Wilson Knight
and L. C. Knights, were far more successful at interpreting and
evaluating dramatic literature because of their knowledge of and
interest in drama on stage. Brooks and Heilman, however, remain
the only New Critical writers who set out to write on playreading.
John Galyean's 1979 dissertation, which applies the poetic theories of New Critic John Crowe Ransom to interpreting playscripts,
fails to mention Brooks's and Heilman's "anthology," which may
indicate a tendency to regard *Understanding Drama* as a textbook
for the classroom rather than as a critical work. However, other
writers, including Gross, Hornby, and Carlson, perhaps because
they encountered *Understanding Drama* first as students and later
as teachers, make a point of discussing it. Their criticism may
reflect a necessary stage in their formulation of their own ideas.

In positive terms the book pointed students and teachers toward
close readings of dramatic texts. Unfortunately, in refusing to define the playscript as a literary genre with an essentially extraliterary component, *Understanding Drama* robbed drama of its hybrid
nature, exiling from the reader's experience what Cocteau called,
in his preface to *Les mariés de la Tour Eiffel,* "theatre poetry" (or
"poetry of the theatre") as opposed to "poetry in the theatre."[26]
The readings that this critical anthology promoted could not adequately account for the role of the stage and of the audience. To
Brooks and Heilman and to those for whom their anthology
formed a major part of the literature curriculum, this weakness
was perhaps not so immediately apparent as the book's considerable strengths.

Rowe and Reading to See

A second key text, *A Theater in Your Head* (1960), is by Kenneth
Thorpe Rowe, a well-known university teacher of playwriting; the
book was "[w]ritten," says the endpaper, "for the theater-lover as
well as the student . . ." Like Brooks and Heilman, Rowe advises
a close reading of playscripts. However, unlike his New Critical
predecessors, Rowe advocates that the reader try, while reading
the playscript, to imagine a fully staged version of the play.

Rowe's insistence on relating the theatrical experience to the
playreading process reiterates what others had already said. For

example, in the classic self-help guide by Adler and van Doren, *How to Read a Book* (first published in 1940), we are told, "a play lacks a physical dimension when we read it in a book. The reader must supply that dimension. The only way to do that is to make a pretense of seeing it acted."[27] Nonetheless, only Rowe manages to bring these ideas to a full-length study of playreading. Rowe never refers to previous critics except for Aristotle, and *A Theater in Your Head* is referred to by only one other writer on playreading. Although Rowe's discussion of playreading is far less sophisticated than Styan's or Gross's, his book is important because it is the first to articulate explicitly the idea of a playreading process.

Rowe makes envisioning a playscript's performance on stage a crucial part of playreading. Early on he poses the problem of reading dramatic texts by comparing playscripts with fiction: "The imaginative responsibility of the reader of a play becomes clear if one considers the proportion in the typical novel given to description of the sights and sounds of the story."[28] The implication here is that the reader needs to take on the task of supplying the visual and auditory aspects of the playscript. For Rowe, the playscript is not wholly dependent on dialogue, as it is for Brooks and Heilman. Instead, the literary form requires the reader to begin by drawing on those elements, both explicit and implicit in the script, that permit the reader to add to the dramatic text a clear sense of the theatre text. Such elements, "the sights and sounds of the story," Rowe tells us,

> are the contributions of the theater and of the creative reader to the text of the play, derived in part from a few lines of stage directions, but primarily from within the body of the play where the quality and being of the characters must be discerned in what they do and say and the total existence and meaning of the play must be found.[29]

In his opening chapter, Rowe declares that playreading is composed of two kinds of activities. In the first the reader constructs from the script an imagined stage performance; in the second, he tells us rather enigmatically, the reader "experiences the play ideally, the scene which it is the function of scenery and lighting to suggest, [and] the characters which it is the function of acting to create."[30] Although he never clarifies this "ideal experiencing," and although his second step sounds more like the realization of the first rather than anything separate from it, Rowe proceeds to state that the reader must first "see" the work and can only then begin to understand it: "[The reader's] experience will be most

complete by an interaction of the two approaches through succes-
sive readings and by a correlated cultivation of literary perception
and acquaintance with the theater."[31] We find, in Rowe's brief,
eight-page introductory chapter, the sketchy beginnings of a discussion of a playreading *process*.

The body of the book, arranged in three sections, tries to illustrate this two-part notion of playreading. In the first section, "Experiencing the Play," Rowe comments at length on the theatre's
physical structure and conventions, and the various stage personnel—producer, director, actor, and the set, costume, and lighting
designers—with whom the playwright must collaborate. In the
second section, "Understanding the Play," are chapters on the
play's meaning, on the relationship of dramatic structure to meaning, and on dramatic genres (tragedy, comedy, etc.); this second
section is amply furnished with examples and illustrations from
well-known plays. In a third and final section, "Evaluating the
Play," Rowe includes the text of *Our Lan'* (1941),[32] "an historical
Negro drama in two acts" by Theodore Ward. On pages facing
the script he gives a detailed running commentary; it provides a
model for readers to follow in their own close readings, which
are, true to Rowe's instructions, sensitive to both the language of
the speeches *and* what happens on stage. The author's close reading of *Our Lan'* offers a hint of some of his affinities with the
New Critics; at the same time, however, his extraliterary concerns
(about the theatre and its traditions) suggest some important differences. Indeed, Rowe's very choice of Ward's play, with its explicitly topical and political references, which lead the reader beyond
or away from the text, reflects a departure from the New Critical
tendency to regard literary works as timeless and apolitical and
to choose texts which substantiate this view.

Rowe does not return to an explicit discussion of his playreading
process until the end of the book, where in a brief overview[33] he
sums up the "Technique of Reading a Play." He reiterates his
initial point about the reader needing to achieve imaginatively a
sense of the play as it would be performed in the theatre, and yet
he almost completely forgets about the second phase of his reading process, except for a vague reference in the book's final sentence: "if the play has the worth and interest to the reader, [then]
comes the analysis, rereading, and development of interpretation
and imaginative projection in one's mind which can lead to a
fuller experience in a subsequent reading."[34]

There are obvious difficulties in Rowe's explanation of playreading. Even if we accept the notion that the reader ought to stage in

his or her imagination a performance while reading a playscript, a problem arises in Rowe's second phase of the two-part reading process, in which "the reader experiences the play ideally, the scene which it is the function of scenery and lighting to suggest, [and] the characters which it is the function of acting to create."[35] Rowe seems here to be suggesting that the successful playreader experiences the fictive circumstances depicted in the play, which is rather different from proposing that the reader become cognizant of the theatre activities that create the fictive world depicted on stage; Rowe seems to be asking the reader to imagine the play as drama but not as theatre.

Rowe's second stage of playreading is thus defined in such a way that we must assume that the performance which the reader imagines communicates without the reader doing anything to respond to it. After the cerebral realization of the dramatic text in performance, Rowe needs to allow for a third phase of reading in which the text, "ideally" experienced through the second phase, is understood beyond what it immediately depicts. In other words, the *meaning* of a play is not identical with its theatrical realization. Does Rowe mean that experiencing the play is the same as responding to it? True, Rowe also mentions analysis and interpretation, but how do they fit into the process as he has defined it?

Another difficulty becomes apparent when Rowe starts to relate plot structure to the definitions of Aristotle:

> For the purpose of a play a unified conflict within the compass of the play is necessary. If the attention of the audience is to be arrested and drawn forward, not thrown back, the conflict will not be under way when the play opens; rather, the play will open on a situation in which the audience is led to see the potentiality of conflict. . . . The course of the conflict follows as a unified sequence, one situation giving rise to the next. . . . Thus we have Aristotle's beginning, middle, and end. . . . As plot grows out of interaction of character and situation the question of outcome, the suspense, for the audience can become focused not on the event or what will happen to a character, but on what the character will do in the situation that has arisen. Just as powerfully, the inner consciousness of the audience is opened and exposed to itself in response to the tension of the play.[36]

Rowe is struggling here with what Aristotle actually wrote, trying, as did Brooks and Heilman, to place the philosopher's ideas of audience reception into an object-oriented framework. To do this, Rowe must turn the spectators into a group who are, for the most part, managed by the play, which (to rephrase the above in active voice) commands their collective attention and leads them to see the potentiality of conflict. Rowe's audience is carried along by the tension of the plot, which focuses them on what the character will do and then opens and exposes them to themselves. As we saw in *Understanding Drama,* when those pieces of the *Poetics* which deal with reception are turned around to conform to the concept of the play as object, the audience is turned into a passive group, capable of only *receiving* the theatrical communication.

Aristotle's resistance to being objectified is most apparent in Rowe's discussion on tragedy. Here, Rowe does not avoid the notion of catharsis (which Brooks and Heilman escape through its translation as "purgation"), but he emphasizes the vagueness and unascertainable meaning of the term as it appears in the ancient "collection of notes," which is "not a finished work." He says that "more important than the pursuit there of implications beyond what can be established is one's own experience of tragedy."[37] Given his objective orientation, we may understand Rowe's sudden shift from what might be deduced from Aristotle's definition of response to one that emphasizes its highly subjective, and thereby imprecise, nature. By so doing, Rowe is able to stave off an otherwise inevitable discussion of response.

Rowe's handling of the concept of catharsis is in harmony with his approach throughout the book. "The basic structure of drama," he tells us, "has developed out of the simple fact that the first business of any play at any level is to get and hold with satisfaction the attention of an audience in a theater."[38] Getting and holding "with satisfaction the attention of the audience" may be more "the first business" of any *playwright* than of any *play,* and we must seriously question the extent to which the audience plays an active role.

Significantly, in his first section about those with whom the playwright has to work, Rowe does not devote a chapter to the audience. In urging readers to imagine the theatrical experience, the author exhorts them to assume the points of view of various theatre personnel—but never that of the audience. Thus he, like the New Critics, in viewing the play as object, presumes the audience's presence. The presumption that the audience is there is so strong that they become a given, transparent to the point of being invisible, and as we inferred from Rowe's interpretation of Aristotle, somehow passive and yet not passive. In Rowe's mental playhouse the auditorium appears to be empty.

Rowe places the reader in an analogously contradictory situation: "It is not enough to be receptive," he cautions, for "a play demands active projection of imagination."[39] In other words, readers must use their minds to let the playscript (which "demands active projection") work upon them. In this manner, Rowe short-circuits his own discussion of the reading process.

I have deliberately deferred any consideration of Rowe's fundamental claim that the reader, in the act of reading, should imagine the play in performance. This idea, which still has substantial currency, is criticized and rejected by Roger Gross and David Grote; I shall therefore address this idea later in this chapter, in conjunction with their books.

Rowe's most famous work remains *Write That Play* (1939), a handbook for aspiring dramatists; moreover, as mentioned above, in his own lifetime he was widely known as a teacher of playwriting. Thus, his concerns in *A Theater in Your Head* perhaps understandably reflect the needs of someone who reads for the purposes of learning to write plays rather than those of a general reader or student who is simply trying to understand a play. Bernard Grebanier's *Playwriting: How to Write for the Theater* (1961), a playwright's manual published just a year after a *Theater in Your Head,* indicates a similar preoccupation with the playscript as the active party in the interaction between the dramatic text in performance and the audience. Grebanier asserts early on that "drama requires the maintaining of unflagging audience interest,"[40] and he later says, "No leisure is permitted the audience to consider or digest what is happening on the stage."[41] With the playwright in control of the auditorium, Grebanier concentrates on explaining what the playscript is and does in formalist terms—what he calls "technique." He even announces, "What we do undertake to teach him [the playwright] is the dramatic form."[42] Although Grebanier does not take up the subject of how to read a playscript, his approach would probably be remarkably similar to Rowe's due to his playwriting, rather than playreading, point of view.

Like Grebanier, Rowe is obviously more interested in the play we read than in our playreading. In Rowe's theatre of the mind, the playscript organizes (with the reader's consent) the dramatic (and to some extent, the theatrical) experience; there is little room for any description of interaction between reader and playscript. Rowe's insistence on adding a sense of the theatrical text to a close reading of the dramatic text marks an obvious improvement over New Critical efforts; in this respect his concept of playreading is far more active and truer to the nature of the playscript itself than that of Brooks and Heilman. Yet, in spite of his theatrical viewpoint, Rowe's explanation of the process of reading plays is only slightly better able to examine the responses of either audiences or readers than that of Brooks and Heilman.

The only writer on playreading upon whom Rowe seems to have had any direct influence is David Scanlan, whose *Reading Drama* (1988) begins with a quote from *A Theater in Your Head*. Scanlan's work is reviewed later in this chapter.

How-To Playreading Books

In the middle of the 1960s, as academic enrollments increased and textbook markets expanded, several student-oriented self-help guides devoted to the reading of playscripts emerged. These were designed for students either bound for college or already enrolled as undergraduates. None of these guides was especially revolutionary or even original, for all were intended to deliver what publishers presumed students needed and wanted: acceptable, conventional critical views shared by university-level instructors.

Some, like Christopher Russell Reaske's *How to Analyze Drama* (1966) and Gary Vena's *How to Read and Write About Drama* (1966), tried to be practical. Others, like Robert F. Whitman's *The Playreader's Handbook* (1966), Thelma Altschuler's and Richard Paul Janow's *Responses to Drama: An Introduction to Plays and Movies* (1967), and G. B. Tennyson's *An Introduction to Drama* (1967), contained more theoretical material. These books disclose, if nothing more, a glimpse of the stasis in the study of reading drama in the United States—a stasis that is made all the more noticeable when these guides are compared with Ronald Hayman's short but often incisive manual for the general reader of a decade later.

Reaske and Vena, true to the tradition of their publishers (Monarch and ARCO respectively), offer readers a crash course in the history of drama and the literature of the theatre. While Vena's guide is more complete and better written than Reaske's, neither can avoid reducing its subject matter as it rushes toward helping students write their critical essay assignments. Thus, Vena capsulizes the *Poetics* in a paragraph in which the dramatic unities are equated with "classicism."[43] The "Brechtian (Epic) Model" is given a page,[44] and complex topics, such as "Poetry *of* the Theatre" and dramatic irony, get two pages each.[45] Reaske, as if assigned to synthesize the assorted views of English teachers, dutifully breaks down Theme into Man and Nature, Man and Society, and Abstract Universals such as death, freedom, and morality.[46] His section on criticism is divided into three issue-based camps: Aristotelian versus Platonic, relativistic versus absolute, and practical versus theoretical. However, if we look at these dichotomies closely, we notice that they are virtually the same.[47]

If Whitman, Altschuler and Janow, and Tennyson come off as more respectable, it is largely because they are not training the reader to compose an acceptable term paper. Still, their guidebooks do tend to address the same standard subjects and ideas that Reaske's and Vena's do, even as they attempt to convey to students some theory-based strategy for playreading. Tennyson suggests, "Read the play through for story and plot . . . let the dialogue flow so that you are carried along with it."[48] In other words, the reader should try to convert playscript into narrative. Whitman, like Rowe and Grebanier, favors form, claiming that subjective interpretation is faulty and that a study of the structure should inform the reader's judgment.[49] Altschuler and Janow prefer seeing or attending a play to reading it, saying, "A play in print is to a play on stage as the orchestral score is to the performed symphony,"[50]—a provocative idea that, sadly, they never develop.

Not one of these books goes beyond stating what each writer feels is (or occcasionally, what ought to be) common knowledge within the academy. Almost twenty-five years later, as a new generation competes for places in college and enrollments once again swell, both Reaske's and Vena's guides have been reissued. The more "serious" guidebooks of the 1960s, though, remain out of print; it is for current writers, who are fluent in the discourse of the late 1980s—such as David Scanlan—to carry on the task of updating current academic handbooks.

In the late seventies, when most of these manuals had been forgotten, British drama critic Ronald Hayman's slim but interesting volume, *How to Read a Play* (1977), appeared in American bookstores. Hayman aimed his book at the general reader rather than at the student struggling through the academy. Even though *How to Read a Play* still seems today a perceptive and often amusing guide, it remains a highly idiosyncratic, rather personal book that for the sake of wide accessibility fails to connect with what literature on playreading there is.

How to Read a Play provides a very short and deliberately unacademic introduction to playreading. As such, it was responsive to a public need of the late 1970s when the student audience was shrinking but sales of mass-market self-help books were expanding. Basic to Hayman's concise guide for the general reader is

the belief that the play [that you read] comes more vividly to life in
your mind if you are alert to the technical problems the director
and actors have in bringing the words to theatrical life and to the
psychological process of translating printed dialogue and stage directions into mental action.[51]

Hayman echoes Rowe, championing the process through which
readers, as part of reading a play, are advised to create theatres
in their heads. Hayman reminds us that plays are not meant to
be read but to be seen—or rather, as Hayman says (quoting Hamlet's "We'll hear a play tomorrow") *heard*. Completing his contrast
between drama and fiction, he adds that when we read a playscript, "we cannot take in more than one impression at a time," but
in performance "we are simultaneously presented with a range of
stage effects and involvements."[52]

Hayman offers comments rather than commentary, remarks
instead of discourse. *How to Read a Play* contains some brilliant
insights: Macduff and Lennox knocking at the porter's gate and
Biff's knocking at Willy Loman's motel room door occasion some
striking observations on sound;[53] Lopakhin's reluctance to propose to Varya and Pope Urban's change of costume (in scene 12
of *The Life of Galileo*) inspire illuminating observations on the uses
of silence;[54] and Hayman's explication of how actors' performances offer solutions to what the reader sees as ambiguities is
quite ingenious.[55] Nonetheless, these points of light flash by without a clearly argued framework within which to shine. The glim-
mers are short-lived, evocative. Like so many other critics who
write around the topic, Hayman never truly illuminates it, and
How to Read a Play only intermittently helps us gaze upon the
process of playreading.

In the end, Hayman's points all boil down to his premise that
the best way to read a play is to "imagine a performance as vividly
as you can."[56] In spite of the pearls thrown to the reader, the book
reiterates the ideas of Rowe's "theatre-in-your-head." Hayman, in-
cidentally, does not discuss any other critics—not even Aristotle.
His short, conversational, and informal guide, though filled with
references to dramatic literature, is—perhaps to keep the general
reader from feeling overwhelmed by references—seemingly
oblivious to any other discourse on playreading or on dramatic
theory.

Hayman's modest 1970s guide, unlike most of those published
in the 1960s, remains enjoyable. Still, his avoidance of other writers, especially his countryman J. L. Styan, places *How to Read a*

Play outside the mainstream of playreading literature and makes it a minor work, though an interesting one.

Styan and Gross: Serious Playreading

Just a year or two before the appearance of the American student how-to guides, English critic J. L. Styan published what at first glance seems a similar self-help manual. *The Dramatic Experience: A Guide to the Reading of Plays,* the only book which Styan devotes to an explicit discussion of playreading, attempts to "offer simple guidance to students faced with the cold text of a play and having no chance to act it themselves or to see it alive in the theatre."[57] The guide was in fact intended for Commonwealth students preparing for the standardized secondary O-Level and A-Level examinations. Thus, like its American contemporaries, *The Dramatic Experience* condenses centuries of theatre history and theory into small, easy-to-read chapters and emphasizes the medium's formal aspects.

Yet here the similarity ends. Styan's text, even as it tries to operate strictly within the examiners' literary canon and to convey conventional information, has been influenced by what Styan calls "the stage-centred reform of drama teaching and appreciation."[58] Hence, there are numerous drawings of stages, plans of theatres, and diagrams that illustrate such theoretical concerns as the "lines of communication" between the novel and the reader versus those between the playscript and reader.[59] It contains a graph of the "ironic contrast in *Juno and the Paycock.*"[60] The book's visual appeal makes good Styan's claim that "the reader of a play must be ready to see and hear in his mind's eye . . ."[61]

Styan goes far beyond Rowe's notions of mental stagings. Indeed, he repeatedly reminds the reader in various ways that the literature of the theatre must be regarded as a dynamic art form, for "the play becomes a physical and four-dimensional thing."[62] Having warned the reader that methods suited to reading fiction and poetry are often "wrongly applied"[63] to the reading of drama, he focuses on the audience's relationship with the playwright, who "must always think of an audience as a group" because "[d]rama is a social activity . . ."[64] Thus, in addition to his assertions that the language of drama "acquires the refreshing property of being *felt,*"[65] Styan maintains that the presence of the audience is vital to the nature of the dramatic text:

Any play depends to an important degree upon the people for whom it is written and their reason for going to the theatre; and the way the play is written for acting and speaking depends upon the theatre in which it is to be performed. These two factors of audience and playhouse are not really separable, of course, and much of the fascination in the study of drama comes from the imaginative excitement of deducing the relative contributions of the "why" and "how" of the theatre, the relation between the written text, the audience and the play's means of presentation.[66]

In effect, Styan is anticipating what Hayman would write in 1977, that in spite of the reader's tendency not to take in "more than one impression at a time," a play is meant for performance and "in performance we are simultaneously presented with a range of stage effects and involvements."[67] At the same time, Styan hints that the audience is an extension of the play and, by implication, an extension of the playscript.

The Dramatic Experience does not move beyond these statements, nor does it discuss other critics—not even Aristotle.[68] As a book on the reading of dramatic texts, then, it gestures toward important theoretical questions which it never really answers. Perhaps such answers lie beyond the scope of this students' guide. Nevertheless, Styan, with his preoccupation with how theatre works is one of the major influences on Roger Gross, who in the section of acknowledgments in his major study of playreading, laments, "In the playscript interpretation proper, I find, alas, only J. L. Styan."[69]

"This book," begins Roger Gross, in his preface to *Understanding Playscripts: Theory and Method* (1974), "is about the difficult art of understanding playscripts. It is the first, I think, that goes to the roots to lay a foundation for a systematic approach to the problem." Gross notes a lack of critical tradition on this topic, remarking, "There are no books to instruct us, at least none which go much beyond Aristotle's . . ."[70] He then poses the question, "[H]ow does one make sense of the marks-on-paper which are the playscript?" and replies, "The answer . . . is to be found in the field of Epistemology, the study of how we know and what we may know."[71] In the ensuing chapters Gross builds carefully upon theories of knowledge to put together an argument for dramatic interpretation. Although this book is the least accessible of those available on playreading, it constitutes the most serious attempt to account for the process of reading dramatic texts.

While Brooks's and Heilman's anthology was written for college freshmen and sophomores and Rowe's guide was intended for a general readership, Gross addresses his book to teachers and students of directing—in other words, to those involved in training for what has become the central role in modern theatre production. In making his book more widely relevant, Gross recommends that every good reader of plays ought to strive to see things from the director's point of view:

> I have found it best to approach interpretation from the point of view of the person who bears the greatest responsibility for a thorough understanding of the playscript, the stage director. It seems to me that the most productive way for anyone to study a play is as the director does, as if preparing to create a full theatrical extension of that script.[72]

As with Styan, this should not be regarded as a development of Rowe's notion that the reader, while reading the script, should imaginatively see and hear a production of the play. On the contrary, Gross later identifies the play produced mentally as

> a *hypothetical* play, not to be confused with the play which will eventually be staged. . . . The hypothetical play is composed of all the inferences the reader draws from his study which are relevant to what must and what may not happen if a play is to be a performance (embodiment, incarnation, realization, etc.) of this script.[73]

We recognize here a generalized description of different reader activities. As if to emphasize that he is talking about *process*, Gross contradicts S. L. Bethell's New Critical insistence that "script reading must 'begin—and end—with the poetry itself,'" by asserting, "Surely the 'poetry' is not merely the words but what they make happen in the reader's mind . . . ."[74] Gross declares that "the 'poetry,' the 'meaning,' and 'hypothetical play,' are mental events evoked by the words, not the words themselves."[75] Nonetheless, what form or shape these inferences can or should take in the playreader's mind remains vague.

Having established this interactive model, Gross, as promised, launches into an epistemological discussion that investigates signification through signals and symbols. This takes him into the realm of words and the question of whether our responses to them are "apt."[76] Gross argues that we inevitably interpret playscripts through our immediate understanding of the "hypothetical play" (which forms an "internal matrix" of meaning or a "context") and through our concepts of the play's location or situation in history (which forms a "historical matrix" of meaning).[77]

He further divides the activity of abstraction into two separate though related acts: actual sense experience and mental conceptualization of what has been sensed.[78]

In spite of his distrust of aesthetics, which "can't help us to respond appropriately to the individual play,"[79] Gross proposes that the work of art functions as an intermediary between artist and audience: "*The physical object or event is merely a medium, not in itself of interest but only as a device for organizing, controlling, and communicating the real interest, and experience of feeling, potentially at many levels, from the purely sensuous to the intellectual*"[80] (italics in original). In the terminology of information theory, there is a sender, a message, and a recipient, and the playscript is merely the message, which "in itself, means nothing." Rather, meaning occurs when readers come into contact with the dramatic text: "To describe a 'meaning of the script,'" Gross maintains, "is not to find meaning in it but to respond to it meaningfully and formulate a response."[81]

Gross goes on to describe how readers derive meaning from playscripts. His description reflects a certain circularity or mutual dependency of sign and meaning:

> [S]igns are not signs until they mean. We attribute significance (ie sign-status) to events when, in fact, we experience meaning as a response to the event. . . . One can't get the meaning except from the sign; one can't see the sign except for the viewpoint of potential meaning. Piaget calls this closed loop the "genetic circle" of meaning.[82]

This closed system of sign and meaning bothers Gross. As noted above, he questions the primacy of the text. Still, he retains a fear that the reader may arrive at an incorrect, or as Gross would say, "inapt," interpretation of the playscript. "We must not," he warns, "slip into the common error of believing that, since no reading is correct in an absolute sense, all readings are acceptable."[83]

In order to support the notion that the subject (the reader) may come up with unacceptable interpretations of the object (with "inapt" readings of the playscript), Gross must find in the object, or rather in what the object makes "happen in the reader's mind,"[84] intrinsic factors that all readers must, or at least should, agree are indisputably *there—there* at least in the sense that they are always part of the experience of reading a particular playscript. To do this, he borrows *parameter,* a term from mathematics, and *tolerance,* a term from mechanics, to describe the playscript's *intrinsic* abilities to control or delimit a reading. Parameter, "that in a variable system which remains constant," and tolerance, "the degree to which factors may vary and still perform their functions in the system,"[85] reflect Gross's attempt to stabilize individual readings while allowing both for valid multiple interpretations and for a model of the reading process in which the text operates in conjunction with (rather than independently of) the reader.

Understanding Playscripts is at times a perplexing book to read, in part because of Gross's perceptions of the critical context in which he writes. He explains that his theory of interpretation began in 1959 when "Rhetorical Criticism" helped him see that playscripts "are not natural objects to be examined as a chemist examines a compound," but rather "the utterance of men, . . . not to be understood except in light of the situation which produced them."[86] Gross's hopes that literary criticism might provide a method for reading playscripts were dashed by his realization that

> in Literary Criticism the response [to the problem of interpretation] was division into dozens of armed camps . . . Myth/Ritual Criticism, Archetypal Criticism, Marxist Criticism, Neo-Aristotelian Criticism, New Criticism, Psychoanalytic Criticism, and so on endlessly.[87]

This description of literary criticism would be more appropriate had he published his book in 1964 instead of 1974. A perusal of the book's bibliography reveals an absence of some of the more relevant theorists of the 1960s and early 1970s. In contrast, Robert Scholes's bibliography in *Structuralism in Literature: An Introduction* (published the same year as *Understanding Playscripts*) lists many works about which we would have expected Gross to have much to say.[88] By 1974 Russian formalists, members of the Prague School, structuralists, semiologists, even Foucault and Derrida, had all appeared in American editions. By 1974 there was a great deal more varied and (more important) more relevant criticism and theory than Gross acknowledges.[89]

Puzzled by this, I wrote to Dr. Gross at the University of Arkansas, asking him to phone me, and thus I came to interview him on why his book seemed to leave out so many significant critical works and to include, if only to criticize, Brooks and Heilman.[90] He explained that when he was writing the book, the New Critics comprised the predominant theoretical opposition to a new method of interpreting playscripts. He further noted that although he had read structuralists, poststructuralists, and semiologists while writing, he wished to avoid what he saw as critical methods that, through predetermining, restricted interpretation.

As he put it back in 1974, "Any method which encourages or enforces certain interpretive conclusions and/or prohibits others is unacceptable."[91] When I rather unfairly pressed him, fourteen years after *Understanding Playscripts* had been published, to describe what he wanted current readers to think about the book's place in the broad context of literary-critical discourse, Dr. Gross after some thought reiterated his desire "to cut through 'isms.'" The whole idea behind *Understanding Playscripts,* he emphasized, was to "develop technique"; the book was intended to be "a tool kit" and "not a manifesto."

Yet, like all who attempt to escape the narrowness and debilitations of theoretical frames, Gross is inevitably dependent on premises which are themselves grounded in theory of some kind. When I mentioned to him that he had much in common with reader-response theorists, he agreed but voiced his objection to being categorized. His aversion to being labeled itself indicates one of his own theoretical fundamentals: Gross seems to believe that theory can transcend its own limitations. But no theory is free of the assumptions upon which it is constructed. As we have seen, Gross condemns Brooks's and Heilman's criticism as "a series of prejudices disguised as observations."[92] Implicit in his criticism of the New Critics is the notion that it is possible for one to free oneself entirely from the kinds of assumptions that contribute to literary theory.

The contradiction in Gross's attempt to liberate himself from prejudice is apparent even in some of his most important and original ideas, which do not have recognizable counterparts in existing theory. For instance, if we go back to his explanations of parameter and tolerance, we find that he locates these within the context of the reading experience not only in the object itself but in what he would identify as the author's intentions as seen via the object:

> An author may create an extensive, precise, detailed parameter for one play and a very limited one for the next. . . .
> The concept of tolerance applies to all aspects of the play. Some scenes must be localized precisely, others, even though the author may specify a location, might occur in any of several locations or in limbo.[93]

True, Gross later defines "author's intention" as "a 'shorthand' way of talking about how things happen to happen which is valuable since men know no way to describe literally what happens in complex mental events. . . ."[94] Yet, even though Gross feels that

author's intention "is no more than a potentially deceptive reifica-
tion of his [the reader's] own process of inference . . . ," he asserts
the reality of the reader's "response to the sign-field *created by the
author*"[95] (italics mine). In present theoretical terms, then, Gross's
position on the contributions of subject and object to the reading
experience is merely one of several that are possible.

I am not claiming that Gross's theory is incorrect (or "inapt"),
but I am suggesting that it *is* a theory, and thus it cannot avoid in
some way constructing itself out of ideas that, as ideas, are susceptible to critical dispute. Thus, Gross may escape being called a
deconstructionist or a formalist, but he cannot, in creating a theory of playreading, avoid beginning with premises that will in
some way influence the kinds of interpretations he can make; in
the illustration given above, for example, his interpretation must
inevitably be influenced by his assumption that the sign field is
"created by the author."

Gross's theory of playreading, then, may explain more than any
of those that precede it, but, as Einstein reportedly remarked to
Heisenberg in reference to quantum mechanics, "it is the theory
which decides what we can observe."[96] Implicit in this remark is
the notion that one cannot see without a theory: theory directs
what may be seen both for better and for worse, enhancing vision
and restricting what is considered visible. Gross may wish to hand
the reader a tool kit, but behind even the simplest set of tools
there necessarily lies some theory of mechanics.

Two additional aspects of Gross's book remain to be explored:
his commentary on Aristotle and his discussion of the audience.
With regard to the *Poetics,* Gross contradicts Aristotelian concepts
of dramatic form by dismissing "*any* absolute standard [as] a rule
'inherent' in drama," and asserting, "Whatever affects a percipient's standards of unity is in the percipient. . . ."[97] Similarly, although he accepts catharsis as an "apt" and meaningful response
to *Oedipus Rex,* he sees an antithetical response, a "disequilibrium,
the unresolved tensions which result from disappointed expecta-
tion of a logical resolution," arising from a play like Weiss's *Marat/
Sade.*[98] In addition to catharsis, Gross finds some of Aristotle's
basic concepts eminently useful. He retains *dynamis,*[99] *praxis* and
dianoia,[100] and agrees that "we understand a dramatic character
by examining the choices the character makes. . . ."[101] Gross says
no books "go much beyond" the *Poetics,*[102] and his relationship to
it is complex.

Complex too is his attitude toward the concept of audience for
the reader of playscripts. In setting a limit to "aspects of meaning-

response" for a playscript, in order to control the subjectivity of the individual, Gross diagrams two "levels" (or perhaps, as his figure suggests, two realms) of meaning, one of which he calls "audience" and the other "rhetorical." The "audience level" of meaning is comprised of that which is

> experienced by a percipient of the play/script. This sort of meaning may be considered from two points of view:
> a) HYPOTHETICAL: what an interpreter believes an ideal audience would experience, a "public" meaning;
> b) FUNCTIONAL: what actual individuals *do* experience in particular exposures to the play/script, a "private" meaning which can never be fully known by an interpreter *or* by the person experiencing it.[103]

Much later in his discussion, Gross looks at the question of Falstaff's cowardice. Here too, the audience, or rather the *idea* of an audience, is proposed as a source for a solution: "As soon as such questions arise, the interpreter should . . . [ask] what happens and how the audience should respond to each event."[104] For, as Gross finally concludes,

> the basic experience of an audience member *is* the experience of characters (admittedly fictional) behaving. To leave the basic experience of the audience out of consideration would be to neglect the interpreter's main task, to behave somewhat like a chef who never tasted the soup. . . .[105]

Gross's suggestions about the audience as an active component in the interaction between reader and playscript, complicated though they may be, nevertheless gesture toward a dimension of playreading that extends beyond the stage and into the auditorium. His remarks here are perhaps among the most important contributions to any study of how the reader of playscripts relates to the notion of the theatre audience.

Overall, *Understanding Playscripts* displays a complexity that makes previous and even most subsequent studies on the topic appear facile. In spite of some of the book's theoretical difficulties, notably its evasion of theoretical affiliation in an attempt to be theory-free, it does not shy away from the act of reading the playscript. Moreover, although Carlson is not wrong in noting Gross's "affinity to such Europeans as Kowsan and Ruffini, who at the same time were developing a modern semiotics of the theatre,"[106] we cannot ignore how Gross occasionally views playreading from a point of view that we might today relate to approaches associated with reception or even reader-response writers.

Dr. Gross expressed over the phone some regret that his book was so, as he put it, "dense." He has felt recently that for a readership of directors or director-educators the work contains material that is not only too abstract but also too unfamiliar. Robert Beath in his 1979 dissertation disagrees: Beath sees Gross's book as the crucial methodological work for those writing on director-oriented script interpretation. In any case, more than fifteen years after its publication, *Understanding Playscripts* remains the central text in the literature of playreading.

Structuralism: Hornby and Gardner

Two writers working after Gross's *Understanding Playscripts* try to use structuralism to rework the concept of playreading. Richard Hornby seriously misconstrues structuralism and consequently produces a book that fails to advance the reading of dramatic texts. Robert Gardner, in his 1983 dissertation, succeeds in prompting questions about playscript interpretation which structuralism seems unable to answer.

Richard Hornby published *Script into Performance: A Structuralist Approach* in 1977, the same year in which Hayman's brief *How to Read a Play* appeared. While Hayman avoids referring to criticism, Hornby goes to the opposite extreme. Hornby has discovered what he calls Structuralism ("and let the capital *S* show that I am definitely not talking about traditional concepts of dramatic structure"),[107] and claims that Structuralism, as he practices it, can solve the major theoretical problems currently plaguing drama and also clear up a good deal of confusion about performance and theatre.[108]

Hornby's structuralism is close to a kind of formalism. In his hands it is nothing more than a methodology which merely redefines form and which "finds the essence of a work in the relation between parts rather than in the parts themselves; these relations form patterns or 'structures' that define what the work truly is."[109] It is perhaps this misreading of the French structuralists (Lèvi-Strauss and Barthes, but not Saussure, whom Hornby never mentions) that prompts Keir Elam, one of the more capable post-structuralist drama critics, to call Hornby's exposition of structuralism "reductive."[110]

In Hornby's hands, structuralism turns into a widely applicable, positive label—a term of praise rather than a critical tool. Chomsky becomes that "Structuralist linguist," and, after synopsizing performance theories by Stanislavski, Brecht, Artaud, and Schechner, Hornby sums up: "all four . . . can be considered in some sense Structuralists. . . ."[111] Perhaps the most outrageous use of the term emerges in Hornby's discussion of the *Poetics*. "Aristotle," he asserts, "was in many ways a Structuralist."[112] It is difficult to take Hornby seriously.

Still, *Script into Performance* depends on this depiction of structuralism for a serious reason: the intent of the book "is to develop approaches to the production of classical playscripts that will be valid, imaginative, and powerful. . . ."[113] Hornby believes that recent productions of Shakespeare and the Greeks demonstrate serious misinterpretations of what the actual playscripts mean. Thus, for him, structuralism offers a way to "prevent some of the zany extremes in production that are becoming all too common. . . ."[114] In other words, he looks to what he calls "Structuralist" theory to render incontestable judgments on dramatic interpretations—*objective* judgments.

Hornby is familiar with Gross's book, or at least knows it to mention, and he pronounces Gross, along with Styan, a structuralist at heart.[115] He inevitably simplifies Gross's notions of playreading and at the same time belittles the New Critics, notably Brooks and Heilman; although such a belittling was perhaps not an uncommon thing to do in the late 1970s, Hornby does little to establish his own thesis. Readers may come away from *Script into Performance* with a preference for Hayman's *How to Read a Play*, which manages to discuss playreading without making wild allegations about other writers.

Although Robert Gardner's "The Dramatic Script and Procedural Knowledge" (1983) does not deal directly or thoroughly with playreading, his dissertation does involve a discussion of the reading of dramatic texts. Gardner asserts (in his abstract) that

> dramatic education at the tertiary [freshman-sophomore college] level should deal, in a focussed way, with the issue of dramatic form as it is manifested by the effective script or text *prior* to moving on to historical surveys, *praxis*, or the consideration of information which is largely extrinsic to the form itself.[116]

In this way he makes obvious early on that he is largely concerned with form. Nonetheless, what Gardner has to say about those who have written on playreading does offer a rather clear understanding of how most of the preceding literature has been construed. This is in itself important because more recent works (Grote and Scanlan, discussed below) fail to pick up the thread of the existing discourse.

The second chapter of the dissertation, Gardner's review of the literature, documents his extensive research, which includes Brooks and Heilman, Gross, and Hornby. Like Hornby, Gardner sees structuralism as a way of getting at hard, indisputable knowledge of playscripts: "What structuralism may have shown us is that we must move beyond opinion and elegant interpretation to data."[117] This statement, advocating an objective appreciation of the playscript, may in fact reflect Gardner's disagreement with Gross, who is uncomfortable with the idea that readers can talk of literature in a genuinely objective way. Gross uses the notion of "elegance"—which Gardner rejects—to explain his ideas of interpretation:

> Scientists use the term "elegance" to describe one of their evidential standards; given two or more possible judgements, the simpler, more coherent, more likely-seeming is to be preferred. Scientists, in fact, have a disadvantage because they actually seek truth; elegance is only an interim standard which must yield to new concrete evidence. *In script interpretation,* however, *the most elegant explanation is correct.* There is no "real-world" meaning. All explanations are open to argument, but inevitably decisions are based on what is known to be best. Physical evidence may alter an explanation by causing the interpreter to see differently, but it serves a different function than the hard physical evidence science occasionally achieves.[118]

We glimpse here a major divergence in thought. Gross, working outside the structuralist movement, argues against the kind of knowledge that Gardner and Hornby seem to find so crucial to reading playscripts. While Gross has profound reservations about the stability of our understanding of the text, Gardner holds fast to the notion that it is the text, not the reader, that actively controls the reading interaction.

Gardner's position begins to remind us of Hornby's when, near the close of his dissertation, Gardner asserts, "Any successful play begs for a response to the questions: why did people *want* to experience this work? What need was fed? Why did it work, and why does it continue to work?"[119] Gardner's questions first assume that the reader can find through his or her readings of the playscript the answers to these questions. Secondly, by claiming that the play "continues to work," they imply that a play works now in the present in the same way it did in the past. Brooks and Heilman, Rowe, and Hornby (and as we shall soon see, Grote and Scanlan too) to a great extent share Gardner's two assumptions. Of all the writers on playreading, only Gross, in spite of his affinities with structuralists and poststructuralists, would regard Gardner's questions, as well as any attempts at definitive answers to them, as suspect.

Instead of looking at things the way Gardner does, perhaps it would be more interesting to ask about the play which in its own day was unsuccessful but which today suddenly seems to "work," or the play that in its own time was a fantastic success but now appears unproducible, unreadable. Or perhaps it would prove more rewarding to wonder about the play which flourishes in a small non-equity house and on the stages of community centers but which flops miserably on Broadway. Perhaps plays like these, even more than what we think of as the great classics (which we assume, often quite erroneously, have always been great successes) beg for a theoretical approach that can help us understand them.

Later Work: Grote and Scanlan

Two recent books, one by David Grote, the other by David Scanlan, carry the literature on playreading into the late 1980s. While each writer proceeds from his own distinct point of view, each has been influenced to some degree by (or at least appears to be aware of) reader-response criticism and reception theory. In spite of this influence, however, both writers' ultimate allegiance to the playscript-as-object blurs some of their own more provocative commentary on how playscripts should be read.

Like Gross and Hornby, Grote's main purpose in his book *Script Analysis: Reading and Understanding the Playscript for Production* (1985) is to "discuss how specific scripts work so that people who need the information for a production can find and use it." He adds, however, that "people who read a script in order to act, direct, design, or produce it must read it in a different way than people who read it for pleasure or to write papers."[120] Thus, Grote disagrees with Gross's suggestion that all good readers would do well to read the playscript as professionals do; his approach appears to accept, if only tacitly, that nonprofessional readers do not (and by implication, need not) read with a heightened awareness of theatre production. This initial contradiction sets the intellectual tone for the book as a whole, which in spite of its acute sense of theatre performance often seems at odds with itself.

Grote's advice to his readership of professionals appears, at least at first glance, to reflect current reader-oriented theory. As if to emphasize playreading as process, Grote instructs us during our initial reading of the playscript, *"Read but do not visualize"* (italics in original). He urges that visualization be deferred until subsequent readings.[121] While this is an interesting idea, we may legitimately wonder just how it is possible to read a playscript (or for that matter *any* work of literature) without forming some mental picture. Is Grote advocating that we avoid making concrete *all* imagery—sounds as well as sights? Or would it be more accurate to infer that he means we should keep our imaginations flexible, changing and adjusting the images our minds summon up in response to the playscript as we read through it? Grote never really clarifies this puzzle.

As a result of what is probably some contact or even sympathy with reception theory, Grote devotes an entire section to script interpretation from the point of view of the play's spectators. This becomes problematic in light of his formalist assertion elsewhere that the script is "complete, in the sense that it tells the reader everything that must be in the performance."[122] His attention to the theatre audience cannot hide the conflict between the topic he has raised and the model on which his theory is based:

> The playwright organizes a script not only to give the audience information about the action and characters but also to have some effect on the audience. Some of this effect will come from the information itself—that is, the action and/or the characters may be interesting in and of themselves. But far more of the effect comes from the way the material is organized.[123]

This model, repeated throughout playreading literature, relies on the notion of the playscript as object; in performance, the play is active, the audience passive, and analogously, the reader too. Even the professional theatre reader, remains for the most part a receptor. Yet Grote, perhaps without even realizing just what he is suggesting, adds, "the playwright seeks to affect the way the audience responds to the play."[124] Interestingly, this statement conveys some awareness that the audience has a mind all its own and that meaning at least in part originates in the audience, as opposed to the playscript.

Nonetheless, Grote is committed, despite the complexities in his own description of audience response, to upholding the primacy of the dramatic text and subordinating the role of the audience. This commitment sometimes leads him in circles:

> [A]n audience is simply the people who are likely to understand a clear production of the information in the script. The audience that a play is designed to affect is precisely that audience in which such an effect occurs.[125] (Italics in the original)

Frequently, Grote's use of language appears to be determined by his theoretical assumptions. "The script," he asserts, "defines the play that the production presents to the audience";[126] here, the text-object and its attributes become the active grammatical subjects, while the subjects (those watching or reading) are transposed into grammatical objects. Grote's abstractions sometimes conflict with his knowledge of how theatre works. As if to clarify his insistence that the playwright's intentions are of foremost importance, he explains:

> Playwrights include information in their scripts to indicate the ways in which the audience should be stimulated and encouraged (or discouraged) in order to produce a reasonably uniform response to the play.[127]

Ironically, this statement, which is no doubt intended to uphold the model Grote has elsewhere described, echoes his earlier remark that "the playwright seeks to affect the way the audience responds to the play." Logically, if the spectators indeed need to "be stimulated and encouraged (or discouraged)" for the sake of response, we may infer that response is not merely a matter of an audience receiving the correct message but more of a dynamic, two-way interplay between what happens on stage and what happens in the house.

Still, Grote sticks with his model. With it, the problematic idea of "a reasonably uniform response to the play" does not have to be considered, nor does the process of response, either by the audience in the theatre or by the reader of the script. Even the idea that there is an audience lurking in the script lies dormant, undeveloped in Grote's object-oriented view. Grote's playreading guide for theatre professionals raises a variety of issues that its author cannot resolve. Although his bibliography includes Styan, Gross, Hayman, and Hornby, Grote never discusses them. His book, like so many others, appears to be initiating a discussion rather than taking part in a dialogue which, when his book was published, had been going on for forty years.

As noted earlier in this chapter, the only writer on playreading who refers to Rowe is David Scanlan, whose *Reading Drama* (1988), a guide for college students, uses a passage from *A Theater in Your Head* as an epigraph to the opening chapter.[128] Writing in the wake of nearly two decades of criticism, Scanlan, like Grote, seems cognizant of current literary theories. His preface notes in up-to-the-minute 1980s academese that his book is "designed to empower readers to respond fully and creatively to drama in print," and to offer "useful tools for sharpening script-reading skills."[129] More importantly, he devotes an entire chapter to the audience.

At the same time, Scanlan manages to focus much of his attention on the same formal aspects of drama that so many other playreading critics, including Grote, emphasize. Thus, his explanation of how the reader of playscripts relates to the audience presents explicitly what Rowe merely implies: "As readers we play the audience's part."[130] For Scanlan, the audience's response is intrinsic to the literary object; as he says of response in his own glossary, "The reader can imagine the *responses* of an audience by noticing what kind of role they are given in the script."[131] The conflict that emerges in Grote's attempt to discuss the audience seems, at least initially, apparent here as well.

However, Scanlan does indicate several ways that the reader may "take the audience's part." The first involves the use of what he calls, borrowing from playwright Peter Shaffer, "the communal imagination":

> Of course, we cannot know how an audience will react to a script until it is performed. But we can know how we as readers react, and we can extend our reactions to include what we know about the tastes, interests, and typical responses of our family, friends, and community. If we go to parties, attend performances or sports events, or spend time in classrooms, we already know a lot about the communal imagination. . . . When we ask the old question, What will people think? we are attempting to envision the communal imagination.[132]

This makes clear just who it is that is seated in Rowe's mental playhouse (or at least in Scanlan's updated version of it). The spectators, if the reader imagines any, see and hear and, more important, *think* like the reader; they thereby respond in a way consistent with the reader's concept of what is appropriate response. Even though Scanlan later adds that "reading drama from an audience point of view simply means seeing it through others' eyes as if it were happening in public,"[133] his earlier instructions clearly suggest that the reader should imagine the views of these "others" (through whose eyes he or she is supposed to see) as essentially similar to his or her own. In this way, the "reasonably uniform response" that Grote mentions is easily achieved because the imagined house is filled with clones of the reader.

Other ways for the reader to relate to the audience come via the playscript itself. "All scripts imply the presence of an audience," Scanlan notes, adding that "many specify the audience's role in the action." Scanlan mentions various conventions, such as the fourth wall (which lets the audience pretend they are invisible), the aside (which lets the audience become the confidant of a particular character), and soliloquy (which lets the audience pretend they can hear a character's silent thoughts). Furthermore, Scanlan mentions the presence of an "audience *in* the dramatic space"— those on stage who in effect become surrogate audiences with whom the spectators may identify. These may include one or more characters who are listeners, a chorus, or actual members of the house who are brought on stage.[134]

Statements such as these make explicit and concrete what Grote only very vaguely and generally proposes: that the audience is an extension of the playscript. We may see Scanlan's shift away from the audience and back to the text not merely as the maneuvering of an essentially object-oriented critic (which it is) but more significantly as a step toward locating what many reader-response critics have called the "inscribed reader" or the "reader in the text." Scanlan's remark that the script specifies the audience's role recalls Wolfgang Iser's assertions that novels describe their own readership. As we will see in the next chapter, Iser's notions are applied to the reading of playscripts by Karen Laughlin, and Scanlan's emphasis toward stage-oriented script conventions is paralleled by a number of semiologists and by Kirsten Nigro.

Conclusion

This survey of what I have called the literature of playreading begins with Brooks and Heilman and to an extent parallels the theoretical progression which followed the New Criticism. Rhetorical criticism, structuralism, and poststructuralism make cameo appearances as writers on the reading of dramatic texts continue to cling to the text rather than embrace the reader or reach out to the interactive process of reading. Nonetheless, at least in its later stages, this literature appears to be growing closer to an acceptance of reader-response and reception theory. It is possible for us to detect some evolution in playreading literature, and we may note how the playreader's concept of theatre audience seems to appear rather late in the course of development.[135]

Over a period of forty-five years, we find writers advising playreaders to invent a narrative thread, to pay attention to the characters' language, to create an image of what is happening on stage and, later, to form a sense of what is going on in the theatre, even in the theatre auditorium. Much of what is recommended in the literature remains excellent advice for reading playscripts.

Of course, Scanlan never explicitly refers to reader-response critics; in fact, except for his epigraphs and attributing a quote to Peter Shaffer, he fails to mention other critics (which is perhaps forgivable in a handbook). He also withholds a bibliography, which in a book for students may have seemed to the publisher unnecessary. Indeed, I have no hard evidence that he intends that a reader familiar with literary theory and the literature of playreading should arrive at the conclusions I have offered above. Yet, there is certainly more than a trace of reader-response theory in his book, which, as I write this, is the latest in a long line of playreading texts.

On the issue of how the playreader encounters the theatre audience, Scanlan has more to say than anyone other than Gross. Whether or not Scanlan's methods, which I have compared to Iser's, are useful for playreading may best be determined by an evaluation of what reader-response critics have had to say about dramatic texts.

3

Playreading and the Reader-Response Critics

Introduction

The formulation of this book's overall focus—the playreader's imaginative construction of theatre audiences—is in large part made possible by what reader-response critics have written over the past quarter-century. The same critics have also influenced my commentary on the body of what I have called playreading literature (evident in my use of terminology such as "playreading process" and "inscribed audience"). By studying them I have been able to observe some important affinities and differences among the primarily object-oriented writers of that literature.

Nonetheless, in spite of all the efforts by reader-response critics to explain the reading of literature, certain questions inevitably arise for which there are no easy answers. If, for example, reader-response critics can offer, especially to teachers of literature, an approach to reading which takes into account the interaction between text and reader, why have so few of these critics discussed the reading of dramatic texts? Does not the emphasis on playscripts in the secondary school and university English curriculum, as well as the widespread use of playscripts in the teaching of the literature of other languages, suggest an area that ought to hold some interest for reader-response critics?

The dearth of reader-response studies on or related to the reading of playscripts has been caused by a number of factors. To some extent, the lack of reader-response drama criticism results from practices which pervade the Anglo-American critical establishment. To a greater extent, however, the "theory" or, to be more accurate, the theoretical grounding which governs the reader-response "school" or "movement," has itself been responsible for the failure of reader-response critics to investigate the reading of dramatic literature.

These debilitating factors are evident from what the major reader-response critics *have* written about dramatic texts and also from what they *have not*. A few critics, whom I call (in the tradition of the theatre) "fringe" reader-response critics, have incorporated some reader-response thinking into their own work. Though they remain interested in exploring the relevance of reader-response criticism to drama, they resist any commitment to or identification with what Kirsten Nigro calls a reader-response "posture."[1] These fringe critics, some of whom position themselves on a borderline between reception aesthetics and semiology, succeed both in clarifying the limitations of reader-response criticism and in pointing toward ways of applying it to playreading. A review of what "mainstream" reader-response critics have written on Aristotle's *Poetics* also confirms that institutional and theoretical impediments have undermined a reader-response investigation of drama.

Before proceeding, I must define a crucial term. In spite of the trend in recent years to think of it as the name of a "movement" or "school," *reader-response* does not readily lend itself to such attempts. A number of writers emphasize the wide diversity among reader-response critics. Robert C. Holub, in *Reception Theory: A Critical Introduction*, defines the American *reader-response*, in contrast to the European *Rezeption*, as "an umbrella term that accommodates systems as diverse as Norman Holland's 'transactive criticism', Jonathan Culler's structuralist poetics, and Stanley Fish's affective stylistics."[2] Jane P. Tompkins, in introducing one of the two anthologies that drew attention to this body of literature, suggests that *reader-response* is necessarily rather general:

> Reader-response criticism is not a conceptually unified critical position, but a term that has come to be associated with the work of critics who use the words *reader, the reading process,* and *response* to mark out an area for investigation . . . . [and who] would argue that a poem cannot be understood apart from its results.[3]

In her introduction to *The Reader in the Text: Essays on Audience and Interpretation* (1980), the other anthology which has come to be regarded as central in popularizing what we know as reader-response criticism, Susan Suleiman avoids the term *reader-response,* using instead "audience-oriented." In so doing she, like Tompkins, admits that such criticism

> is not one field but many, not a single widely trodden path but a multiplicity of crisscrossing, often divergent tracks

and that her intent is to map

> however tentatively, the principal tracks in the landscape—not in order to simplify them or minimize their diversity.[4]

One important aspect, then, of reader-response criticism is that it consists of a wide variety of writings, many of which under other circumstances would be viewed as belonging to very different schools of literary criticism.

Still, it would be less than honest to deny that over the past twenty-five years there has been, if not a movement, then a general move toward replacing, as Steven Mailloux in *Interpretive Conventions* puts it, "examinations of a text-in-and-of-itself with discussions of the reading process, the 'interaction' of reader and text."[5] Furthermore, as Elizabeth Freund in *The Return of the Reader* insists, an inescapable consequence of such a replacement is the institutionalization of a whole new kind of study: "By refocusing attention on the reader instead of the text as the source of literary meaning, a new field of inquiry is opened up."[6] We must therefore look at some of the writings that have in some way opened the field of reader-response literature. Unlike the body of playreading literature, which I have argued does exist, it seems the invention of those who write the criticism itself and also of those who write about it, both pro (such as Suleiman) and con (such as Freund).

Although a complete survey of the body of reader-response criticism is beyond the scope of this book, an explanation of what I mean by *reader-response* is clearly in order. Throughout this study, I use *reader-response* loosely, frequently with relevance to an interactive model that is occasionally only implicit in what many of the so-called reader-response critics offer. I apply the term to contemporary writers who in some way scrutinize the relationship between text and reader. While I recognize that there is perhaps no single critic who may represent reader-response critics at large, there is undoubtedly what we can and must call reader-response criticism, and from this body of literature we can begin to detect in the work of one writer or another *tendencies* that are representative of reader-response criticism and its treatment of drama.

The Reader-Response Evasion of Drama

It would be difficult for any English-language literary critic to avoid drama. With Shakespeare's work commonly acknowledged

as the best in English, reader-response critics, who are interested
both in the reading of literature and (from Richards and Rosenblatt onward) in the teaching of it, have not been able to ignore
dramatic texts. Nevertheless, this body of critical literature does
avoid any sustained discussion of the reading of playscripts. Not
one of those whom we may associate with reader-response critici-
sim—Iser, Fish, Holland, Bleich, Tompkins, Rosenblatt, Riffaterre,
Poulet, Culler, and Richards—has chosen to devote a major effort,
in the form of a book or even an extensive article, on how to read
playscripts.

A good way to begin a discussion of this literature is to examine
a representative reader-response work that does in some way address playreading. The essay that I have chosen is the only one
included in Susan R. Suleiman's and Inge Crossman's *The Reader
in the Text* which discusses drama. (None of the pieces in Tompkins's anthology touches on this subject.) In "'What's Hecuba to
Us?' The Audience's Experience of Literary Borrowing," Peter J.
Rabinowitz tries to explain how readers respond to material which
they have encountered elsewhere in their reading. Rabinowitz discusses Alain Robbe-Grillet's borrowings in *Les Gommes* from *Oedipus Tyrannus* and Tom Stoppard's use of *Hamlet* in *Rosencrantz and
Guildenstern Are Dead*. Thus, Rabinowitz is obliged to give some
account of the difference between reading novels and reading
playscripts.

Attempting to describe the relationship between author and
audience, Rabinowitz utilizes a terminology which he has evolved
from his reading of fiction. He proposes no fewer than three
fiction-reading audiences. The first he calls the *actual* audience,
"the flesh-and-blood readers . . .," the study of whom "is properly
the province of sociological or psychological criticism. . . ." Next
he mentions the *authorial* audience, the readership whom authors
address while they are writing.[7] Finally, he brings up "the narrator
(implicit or explicit) [who] is generally an imitation of an author."
This imitation author, he says, "writes for an audience—an imitation audience that I call the *narrative audience*." There is perhaps
a sound basis for Rabinowitz maintaining such a notion about
fiction; at least he neatly illustrates his theory using Dostoyevsky's
The Possessed.[8] In any case, as his book, *Before Reading: Narrative
Conventions and the Politics of Interpretation* (1987), which deals almost exclusively with novel-length fiction, and his essay on Ray-
mond Chandler's *The Big Sleep* demonstrate, Rabinowitz seems far
more at home with the novel than with the playscript.[9]

In extending his notions on audience to the reading of dramatic
texts, Rabinowitz encounters some perhaps predictable difficulties:

Drama, of course, does not have a narrator in the way that narrative fiction does (although *Travesties* and Anouilh's *Antigone* come close). But even though the dynamics are slightly different (drama imitates the fictional event itself, while a narrative imitates an account of it), there is the same triple role for an audience watching a performance too.[10]

Do Alan Carr in *Travesties* and the Chorus in *Antigone* really "come close" to becoming narrators in the same way that characters do in narrative fiction? Superficially, they may resemble narrators in a story or novel, addressing the audience directly and relating summations of action and theme. That the Chorus remains omniscient and Carr proves unreliable only strengthens Rabinowitz's assertion, for such variations are well-known among the narrators of novels.

Yet, even without applying the very precise vocabulary of narration and narrators which Gerard Genette develops, we may quickly point to serious flaws in Rabinowitz's proposition. The narrator in fiction supplies the text through language (or as Rabinowitz would have it, through language supplied by the author). In drama, however, the words of a particular character (including Stoppard's Carr and Anouilh's Chorus), even if they sound like narrative discourse, are inevitably framed within the play, that is, within the playscript or dramatic text, and must therefore be regarded as dialogue. Perhaps the closest equivalent in a playscript to the sort of narrator that Rabinowitz identifies in fiction is apparent in those words that the theatre audience never hears—those which appear in the stage directions. It is here, in fact, that the reader, not the audience member, may sense Rabinowitz's authorial surrogate, that strong voice which in some way does "narrate." If for example, there is, in Rabinowitz's sense of the term, a *narrator* in the script of *The Glass Menagerie,* it is not Tom but the owner of that all-knowing voice which offers set descriptions and provides details about the action and speeches.[11]

Obviously, a major obstacle to Rabinowitz's discussion of drama is his commitment to narrative fiction, the genre with which he is most familiar. This is directly evident from his attempt to adapt his troika of novelistic narrative-fiction audiences to dramatic texts. Rabinowitz's transfer of the rules governing the reading of one genre to the reading of another exemplifies a ploy that is common throughout modern criticism.

In *Literary Theory: An Introduction,* Terry Eagleton suggests that literary critics frequently tend to make one literary form typical of literature in general. Eagleton notes how the New Critics propagated the concept that all literature is very much like poetry. "Most literary theories," he concludes, "in fact, unconsciously 'foreground' a particular literary genre, and derive their general pronouncements from this. . . ." In other words, a particular type of literature operates, within the context of a theory, as "a paradigm."[12] As Eagleton reminds us, I. A. Richards (who, in addition to being regarded as a New Critic, is often cited as the first reader-response theorist) derives his general pronouncements from poetry. Like Rabinowitz, critics such as Wayne Booth and the Leavises base much of their view of literature on their study of fiction.

Critics, regardless of their critical label(s), may explain that they, like most readers, have a preference for or a greater knowledge of one particular literary genre. Thus, if we look at Louise M. Rosenblatt's use of the concept of the poem in *The Reader, the Text, the Poem: The Transactional Theory of the Literary Work,*[13] we find that her very choice of terminology reflects what Eagleton would call her attempt to "foreground" the poem as a paradigm for all literature. We can detect something very similar in the majority of the essays by Stanley Fish that are collected in *Is There a Text in this Class?* (1980).[14] Likewise, Iser, in what he entitles *The Act of Reading: A Theory of Aesthetic Response,*[15] discusses virtually nothing other than fiction.

But if reader-response critics do tend to build their theories on one literary form, how is it that the playscript is never their preferred genre? To answer this question, we must look to the academic tradition evident in Brooks and Heilman, the tradition in which most reader-response critics were originally trained. It decrees that playscripts are only *partially* literary and that only the *linguistic* elements of playscripts are deemed truly worthy of *literary* consideration. Thus, to base a theory of *literature* on a hybrid or bastard literary form would diminish the model and weaken the theory. According to this line of thinking, one would do better to apply the properties of what is properly called literature to drama. And therefore, one does.

If we return now to Rabinowitz's comments on drama as narrative, we may observe how another misconception emerges in his parenthetical statement that "drama imitates the fictional event itself, while a narrative imitates an account of it." On the surface this sounds reasonable, for many (though certainly not all) playscripts are supposed to represent or depict, and in this sense imitate, action. On a more profound level, however, drama (from the Greek verb *draō*, "I do") is not so much an *imitation* of an action as it is in itself an *enactment,* albeit one that sometimes represents and thereby parallels the outward form of other actions. In responding to traditional, realistic, and avant-garde plays, any audience (whether spectators or readers) must constantly differentiate between the alleged action which "imitates" action (or to put it more precisely, which is a *mimetic* action) and the actual action (of which the mimetic action is only one component) that is taking place on stage.[16]

Rabinowitz appears to have some sense of the immediacy of drama and its own sense of action when, in a footnote, he assumes that the audience viewing a modern rendition of the *Electra* myth in Sartre's *Les mouches* becomes involved in its present enactment instead of regarding what they see as a reenactment.[17] Nevertheless, his assertion that "drama imitates action" fits his theory of three audiences far better than it describes how people (spectators or readers) respond to plays.

I use *plays* in the previous sentence rather than *playscripts* because Rabinowitz himself suddenly shifts from an audience of readers to an audience of spectators: "even though the dynamics are slightly different . . ., there is the same triple role for an audience watching a performance too." This theatrical audience may become what he calls the "narrative audience." Rabinowitz argues that

> in viewing Sophocles' *Antigone* we must not only be our real selves, but must also try to become those hypothetical viewers addressed by the playwright (temporarily sharing their beliefs about burial), while we simultaneously pretend to react to the characters as real people.[18]

Having already indicated the problems inherent to defining drama as a narrative genre, I should add that Rabinowitz is, in advancing his argument, incorrectly assigning which audience it is that "become[s] those hypothetical viewers addressed by the playwright"; in his own terms, that audience is inevitably the authorial, *not* the narrative audience. But, even after such a revision has been made, we may seriously question whether or not theatre audiences do play the sort of role Rabinowitz assigns to them.

However, these matters are relatively minor in comparison with the enormous and unexpected leap that Rabinowitz takes from an audience of readers to an audience of spectators. Like the prisoner whom the Inquisition abandons to the State for execution, the playreader is suddenly dropped from Rabinowitz's discussion and expected to disappear. Indeed, through the rest of his essay, Rabinowitz consistently relates the *reader* of fiction to the *spectator* of a play. This tactic of treating the playreader as nonexistent is common throughout reader-response literature; those few reader-response critics who do comment on plays take startlingly similar leaps. Perhaps the most obvious example of such an evasion is Iser's 1981 essay on *Waiting for Godot* and *Endgame*. In "The Art of Failure: The Stifled Laugh in Beckett's Theatre," Iser, a writer who has written lucidly on the reader of fiction, aims his attention at the spectator, *never* at the reader of Beckett's plays. Iser's essay avoids reader-response criticism by jumping immediately into theatre reception.[19]

There are numerous other, less glaring instances. David Bleich, in *Subjective Criticism* (1978), in referring to an unpublished dissertation by Susan Elliot on Pinter,[20] discusses responses to drama as if reading and seeing a play were the same—that is, without making any attempt to differentiate viewing a play from playreading. This notion may be inherent to Elliot's study—Bleich's quote from her dissertation implies as much—but Bleich himself appears unaware that response inevitably varies between stage and page.[21]

Rosenblatt, in *The Reader, the Text, the Poem*, describes the poem as event and offers what at first appears to be an important distinction:

> To illustrate the reading process, I shall sometimes refer to the texts of plays. The complaint, "Plays are to be acted, not read" may suggest itself. Without rejecting the idea that plays are usually written to be ultimately acted, I still insist that *before they are acted they must be read*—first by the author evoking his intended work and, second, by the director and the actors, who before they interpret must go through the process that I hope to illuminate further in coming chapters.[22]

On the surface, Rosenblatt's statements seem reasonable; she does not really contradict the claim that plays are to be acted, for according to her the proper readers of plays are those involved in production. But she does leave out the nonprofessional readers—the "general" and, most perplexingly, the student playreader—with whom her book is supposedly most concerned. Unfortunately, her "coming chapters" fail to light a clear approach for the reader who is not connected with the theatre but who wishes to read playscripts.

Finally, Norman Holland, in *The Dynamics of Literary Response* (1968), spends considerable effort on the question, "How does Brecht affect us compared to [sic] Ionesco?"[23] Although his discussion is interesting, it is not immediately clear whether "us" refers to an audience of readers or an audience of spectators. Eventually, we locate clues that indicate which of these he has in mind: "Ionesco," he notes, "presents us with a seemingly nonsensical world onstage,"[24] and he later adds, "At a Brecht play, alienation there may be between actors and audience so that we disbelieve the fiction we see. . . ." Holland's subsequent conclusion distinguishes between the "reader," and, the "member of the audience,"[25] and specifies that the "we" of the last five pages refers to "we spectators."[26] What Holland manages here is the same sort of evasion we have witnessed in Bleich, Rosenblatt, and Rabinowitz.

Rabinowitz's essay illustrates a number of trends away from playreading that we may detect throughout much of the reader-response critical literature. Eagleton's notion of a prevalent genre, by which critics choose a particular form of literature to be paradigmatic of literature as a whole, has obviously helped or even encouraged reader-response theorists to avoid playscripts. Furthermore, the nature of the dramatic text, especially its crucial connection to the extraliterary theatre text, has only strengthened the aversion toward drama which critics who are primarily *literary* in orientation may already have acquired. It also makes sense that critics whose primary interest is in literature should know less about the theatre and dramatic literature than about poetry and fiction. These factors contribute to the otherwise inexplicably hasty jumps many reader-response critics make away from the reader of play scripts, and, more important, away from the reading, of playscripts.

We should recall from the previous chapter that body of work written on playreading by more traditional commentators. Reader-response critics, in spite of their differences from (and with) their predecessors, in fact have much in common with other contemporary literary critics. As I have pointed out, Tompkins, an important voice in the reader-response dialogue, is well aware that reader-response critics derive much of their theory and methodology from the very critics from whom they separate themselves. Indeed, the "debt" that Tompkins says reader-response critics owe their formalist predecessors is, she maintains, the ultimate goal of all modern critics, formalists and receptionists alike: "to specify meaning," says Tompkins, is modern "criticism's ultimate goal."[27] Exactly where and how meaning occurs is, of course, very much a matter of dispute. Still, like the New Critics, reader-response critics pursue the significance of literature in the context of establishment academia. They are therefore susceptible to some of the same limitations that have prevented other critics from discussing playreading.

Mary Louise Pratt, in a lucid critique of this reader-oriented strategy, accuses reader-response criticism of taking an "anti-theoretical stance invoked to uphold a neo- or covertly formalist practice. . . ."[28] Whether or not this charge is deserved, the point remains that in spite of their denunciations of the New Criticism, reader-response critics—as their name indicates—are largely concerned, like their critical predecessors, with words on a page. Even with poetry or fiction as their theoretical paradigm, they rarely discuss the listener's response to the poem recited aloud or to the story told by the storyteller. When they are not applying the poetic or fictive form to the playscript, they have no problem in conceding that drama is best encountered in the theatre, and of course, as soon as the dramatic text transfers from page to stage, it falls beyond what reader-response criticism is required to explain.

There is, in addition, yet another possible explanation for this absence of reader-response criticism on drama. Una Chaudhuri, in an essay that is largely semiological in orientation, takes time to examine reader-centered theory and to observe,

> The preponderance of words like "event," "participation" and "happens" in Fish's discourse, as well as words like "performance," "activity" and "process" in the discourse of reader-response criticism in general, would lead one to expect this criticism to be particularly suited and productive in the study of drama.[29]

Chaudhuri's close reading of the language used by reader-response critics may lead us to conclude that such critics in fact turn what Iser calls "the act of reading" into something that is in itself heavily dramatic. Thus, in the reader-response "theatre-of-the-mind," drama or at least dramatic action becomes the metonymic equivalent of reading itself. This may help explain why Holland and Elliot so readily identify the reader with the spectator; this may further enhance our understanding of why, as Chaudhuri puts it, "the drama is conspicuous by its absence of reader-oriented criticism."[30]

Fringe Critics and Beyond

The reader-response criticism that is perhaps most valuable to a discussion on drama comes not from well-known reader-response theorists but from writers whose work may be located on the fringes of the reader-response literature. These writers are more willing to dispense with some of the rules which limit the mainstream critics and seem more skeptical of the assumptions which reader-response theorists bring to their readings of reading.

Of the "fringe" essays which successfully examine playscripts, the best and most comprehensive is Kirsten Nigro's "On Reading and Responding to (Latin American) Playtexts" (1987). Perhaps the reason Nigro encloses *Latin American* in parentheses is that, although she eventually does discuss reading Latin American plays, the first five pages of her article map out, if only in sketch form, the theoretrical terrain explored by recent reader-response and poststructuralist critics. Aware that her essay does not provide sufficient room to develop her inquiry fully, she raises a number of vital issues, some of which she is unable to resolve. One such issue concerns the reasons that reader-response criticism has neglected drama, a matter which I have tried to explain in the previous section of this chapter.

In addition to Nigro's piece, there are several other fringe reader-response essays: Stephen Booth's "On the Value of *Hamlet*" (1969)[31]; Mardi Valgamae's "Drama as an Art Form: Four Critical Approaches" (1981)[32]; and Karen Laughlin's "Beckett's Three Dimensions: Narration, Dialogue, and the Role of the Reader in *Play*" (1985) and "'Looking for sense . . .': The Spectator's Response to Beckett's *Come and Go*" (1987).[33] These articles, along with Nigro's, chart tentative but nonetheless trailblazing courses through what might otherwise be a desert landscape.

However, before taking up these essays, it is important to glance briefly at the semiological literature on the audience's relationship to the dramatic text, in part because semiologists have played an active role in discussing this relationship and in part because what they have written has had a positive impact on some of the fringe writers.

A number of recent articles, such as Una Chaudhuri's "The Spectator in Drama/Drama in the Spectator" (1984), Shoshona Weitz's "Reading for the Stage: The Role of the Reader-Director" (1985)[34] and Tim Fitzpatrick's "Playscript Analysis, Performance Analysis—Towards a Theoretical Model" (1986),[35] appear to approach the topic of playreading but do so from a semiological (rather than from an overtly reader-response) point of view. Semiological criticism has remained somewhat separate from the largely Anglo-American academic literature; it is for the most part related to a European-based movement. However, while semiology does offer a body of literature on reading the dramatic text that is both larger and more developed than that offered by reader-response criticism, I believe that the science of signs is far less capable of assisting in the sort of examination in which this study is engaged, namely of how playreaders envision theatre audiences.

As Nigro admits, "drama poses some unique and thorny questions for reader-response critics."[36] She adds in a note that "[m]any of these questions have, however, been a major concern in recent theatre semiology, which has turned its attention more and more to the pragmatics, rather than just the classification of sign production . . . ." Although, as Nigro adds, semiology, like reader-response criticism, consists of varied points of view, those within this field do indeed share some common ground, most notably their interest in the sign. Nigro cites Anne Ubersfeld as one of several semiological critics interested in theatre reception and audience interpretation; Nigro's wording here, however, possibly betrays her own reservations about semiology: "efforts are made to try to account for the reception tasks and interpretive abilities of the audience member."[37]

Suleiman, in surveying semiology, derives a series of questions that the "semiotic variety of audience-oriented criticism allows one to formulate . . ."

> How (by what codes) is the audience inscribed within the system of a work? How does the inscribed audience contribute to the work's readability? What other aspects of the work, whether formal or thematic, determine readability or intelligibility? Finally, and in a slightly different perspective, what are the codes and conventions—whether aesthetic or cultural—to which actual readers refer in trying to make sense of texts and to which actual authors refer in facilitating or complicating, or perhaps even frustrating, the reader's sense-making abilities?[38]

All of these questions, which would obviously be useful in any attempt to discuss the playscripts we read, are nevertheless impelled by a theoretical orientation that favors the text rather than the audience or reader. The audience may "contribute to the work's readability," but it is "inscribed within the system of the work." True, "actual readers refer" to codes and conventions "to make sense of texts," but can semiology go beyond expressing what those codes are? Can semiological reception move toward articulating *what the playreader does?*

My answer is that semiological critics are perhaps capable of moving toward the reader or individual audience member, but the closer they come, the more likely they are to lose sight of that which makes them semiologists—their commitment to the sign. I deduce this from the progression Ubersfeld makes from *Lire le théâtre* (1977) to *L'école du spectateur* (1982); in the latter, the shift of interest, from text to spectator, is particularly evident in the book's last two chapters, "Le travail du spectateur" and "Le plaisir du spectateur," in which the audience member becomes a vital part of her discussion on theatre performance.[39] Much of what Ubersfeld says about the spectator concerns his or her relating to the sign systems of the dramatic text, the performance, or the theatrical context; she does, however, describe some individual and emotional response processes which the audience member experiences.

I see a similar progression in Patrice Pavis's work, "Towards a Semiology of the Mise En Scène" (published in English in *Languages of the Stage*, 1982), which traces the realization of the play from the dramatic text through the director's "metatextual" achievement of the performance before an audience, thereby including the spectator as part of the production. I see it as well in Martin Esslin's *The Field of Drama: How the Signs of Drama Create Meaning on Stage and Screen* (1990), in which the very title succinctly sums up a semiological view of the theatre. While Esslin is able to discuss, for example, how each individual audience member has an individual response to a performance,[40] he is ultimately fixated on the performance itself. For Ubersfeld, Pavis, and Esslin that network of signals, the text (whether performance text or literary text), remains central.

As Nigro puts it, "efforts are made." Yet as long as the *sign* is the primary focus of interest, the audience (spectators or readers) must be viewed in relation to it or as functions of it. To transcend totally this focus on the sign would be to exit semiology, which is not, as Nigro says of reader-response criticism, "a theoretical posture" or stance,[41] but more a genuine methodological (or, at least, theoretical) school. That we can talk about "semiological reception" at all should remind us that the labels we employ in discussing theory have serious limitations and that many critics burst (or at least strain the bounds of) the theoretical categorizations in which we place them (or they place themselves). Still, because of the meaning we give the label "semiology" and because the "science of signs" appears to be a coherent movement, I believe this study of the playreader's concept of spectators requires a theoretical "posture" or "stance" which allows critics to move even closer to the reader.

The earliest reader-response work on drama, Stephen Booth's "On the Value of *Hamlet*," was originally presented at the Columbia University English Institute in 1968 (and published in *Reinterpretations of Elizabethan Drama: Selected Papers from the English Institute* in 1969). In his foreword to the collection, Norman Rabkin calls Booth's essay "a controversial reading."[42] Rabkin had earlier indicated that the papers were influenced by recent critical works concerned with the audience, including Fish's *Surpris'd by Sin: The Reader in Paradise Lost* and Barbara H. Smith's *Poetic Closure.*[43]

The context for Rabkin's remarks is important. Lest we imagine that this English Institute more than two decades ago was aware that it had planted the seeds of what we now know as reader-response criticism, we should heed Rabkin's own description of what the volume's contributors were doing:

> Ultimately it [a discussion of the relation between text and reader] assumes it demands a full psychological account of the viewer himself, but strikingly the authors share an interest above all in the object itself as the means to that account, and do not attempt what may in fact not be possible to achieve. Agreeing that their concern with a play is to a great extent a concern with its audience, they seem to agree also that the new concern is best served by a new kind of scrutiny of the play itself.[44]

Rabkin clarifies that the species of criticism blooming here is what we now know as rhetorical. In terms of what would become known as reader-response criticism, Booth's discussion of Hamlet approaches what Steven Mailloux in *Interpretive Conventions* characterizes as Wolfgang Iser's "phenomenological criticism" and Stanley Fish's "affective stylistics."[45]

In his essay, Booth promises to "look at *Hamlet* for what it undeniably is: a succession of actions upon the understanding of an audience." He offers the proposition that the audience is at first confused about the sentinels in the opening scene and that the dialogue reveals that the action in the scene has something to do with the appearance of an apparition. Just as Bernardo is about to describe the ghost, the ghost in fact enters. "The description," insists Booth, "is interrupted by a repetition of the action described." The ghost's entrance, however, both fulfills and frustrates our expectations: it is what we expect and desire, an action to account for our attention to sentinels; it is unexpected and unwanted, an interruption in the syntactical routine of the exposition that was on its way to fulfilling the same function.[46]

Mailloux links Booth's identification of fulfillment and frustration to the "expectation-disappointment structure in the temporal reading model" which Fish finds in *Paradise Lost* and which Iser identifies in *Joseph Andrews*.[47] Indeed, it is the consistent frustration of the audience's expectations and the resultant ongoing apparent lack of coherence, out of which the audience is nevertheless able to make coherent sense, that Booth finds throughout the tragedy.

"On the Value of *Hamlet*" is a remarkable essay; written without the turgid precision of scientific discourse which would soon overrun literary criticism, it articulates elegantly an ingenious interpretation, one that quite deliberately sets out to contradict the affective fallacy: "it is reasonable to talk about what the play does do," asserts Booth, "and to test the suggestion that in a valued play what it does do is what we value."[48]

At the same time, Booth's frequent references to the audience never specify who this audience is. "The first thing an audience in a theatre wants to know is why it is in the theatre,"[49] Booth maintains. But is this a modern audience, an Elizabethan audience, *all* audiences? "As the audience listens [to Bernardo speak of the ghost], its understanding shifts from one system of pertinence to another. . . ."[50] Is this the only inevitable response to the dramatic text? Do not the actor and director have some role in encouraging response, or, perhaps more important, do not an audience's specific circumstances play a strong role in their own determination of what they see?

These are perhaps obvious—and rather unfair—questions. Instead of belaboring Booth's use of the first person plural to stand for *audience*, it is better to emphasize his definite move away from the New Critical perspective that is evident in Brooks and Heilman and even in Rowe, which in a way viewed the auditorium as empty. Even if we (and here I mean "we readers") disagree with Booth's interpretation, his methodology opens the door to a wide range of questions and concerns. These questions and concerns are perhaps most evident in the recent work of several critics who, even as they read playscripts with reference to a vague and generalized audience, express at least on a theoretical level a sometimes stunning recognition of the audience's role. Indeed, in William Gruber's *Comic Theaters: Studies in Performance and Audience Response* (1986)[51] and Stanton Garner's *The Absent Voice: Narrative Comprehension in the Theater* (1989), the introductory material on the audience is rather dazzling, but the criticism that follows does not go beyond Booth's in its ability to identify and discuss audience response. Similarly, Sidney Homan, in *The Audience as Actor and Character* (1989),[52] prefaces his lucid readings of modern dramatists by stating his interest in "the concept of audiences" as indicated by the playscript, as if audiences were merely functions of the script itself.

Perhaps the best way to view Booth's trek through the tragedy is to regard it as following only one of many possible pathways. With this in mind, we may begin to chart our own related but different routes.

Two essays by Karen Laughlin, "Beckett's Three Dimensions: Narration, Dialogue, and the Role of the Reader in *Play*" and "'Looking for sense . . .': The Spectator's Response to Beckett's *Come and Go*," follow the presentation of Stephen Booth's paper by more than a decade. Laughlin views *Play* as "a radical experimentation with narration and dialogue [which] reasserts and builds on the fundamental role of dialogue as a constituent element of the dramatic form." Connecting the use of the spotlight in the play to the role allotted the audience and reader throughout the script, she compares the spotlight to "Wolfgang Iser's 'wandering viewpoint', which permits the perceiver 'to travel through the text', while at each moment presenting the 'only segments of textual perspectives' which the reader/spectator must synthesize."[53] In this essay, Laughlin begins to put together an Iserian approach to playreading.

In "Looking for sense," Laughlin further develops some of Iser's ideas and adapts them to the reading not of fiction but of dramatic texts. Basing her analysis on Iser's theory of aesthetic response, Laughlin looks at Beckett's *Come and Go* in order to find "the role laid out for the reader by the text itself" and "the conditions that bring about its possible (or potential) effects."[54] She adds that "many of the textual strategies of *Come and Go* are related to its orientation toward performance and should work to guide the responses of the armchair reader and the theatre spectator alike." Thus she revises Iser's "implied reader" to the "implied spectator."[55]

Laughlin proceeds along Iserian lines, identifying numerous indeterminacies (textual ambiguities or vaguenesses which the reader must fill in) and commenting on the resonance of specific allusions.[56] These theoretical borrowings yield interesting results. Unlike Stephen Booth, Laughlin is able to foresee and thus account for variant responses: "the most vocal respondents. . . ," she tells us, "are likely to become fully engaged in this composition process [of making sense of an overdetermined text]"[57] and "[s]uch an approach . . . further suggests that a response of either bemused or angry silence may be equally due to the text's overwhelming indeterminacy."[58] In keeping with Iser, Laughlin allows that many responses are possible. She has little sympathy for Wayne Booth's remarks (she says he sees Beckett as "potentially boring and also fundamentally nihilistic") but she says, "I do not wish to deny this as a valid response."[59] This is a far cry from Stephen Booth's rather singular description of what the audience does in unison during given moments of *Hamlet*.

However, like Stephen Booth (who, as we noted above, has much in common with Iser), Laughlin never names her audience; her spectators, diverse though they may be, are very much "implied" by the text. Even with the notion of response expanded beyond the monolithic reactions of Booth's spectators of *Hamlet*, Laughlin's spectators remain idealized spectators or rather personifications of her ideas on possible responses. And just as Booth's essay suggests that he is describing *all* audiences' responses, so in fact does Laughlin's—and hers does so far more convincingly, for she (in keeping with Iser's pluralism) is able to approach the topic with a theory and terminology which sound more exacting than Booth's and which seem to let her describe more than Booth is able to. Her conclusion emphasizes the scientific nature of her role as literary critic:

> [A]s the preceding analysis of responses to *Come and Go* suggests, an audience-oriented approach need not choose from among seemingly contradictory responses to the play, nor must it insist on seeking a "correct" and "affirmative" interpretation of works like this one. On the contrary, a criticism focussed on the *process* of audience response, and on the role of the dramatic text in guiding this process, may help free literary studies from the contradictions and limitations of an ethically-motivated approach . . . ; at the very least, such a criticism can more precisely and effectively account for both the excitement and the discomfort characterizing the spectator's experience of Beckett's dramatic works.[60]

The "contradiction and limitations" inherent in what this sort of ciriticsm can do "at the very least" remain rather troubling. Booth, Iser, and Laughlin purport to describe audience response without talking about the specifics of the audience; in short, they continue to scrutinize the text, thereby making good Tompkins's claim that reader-response critics bear a resemblance to their New Critical forbears. Laughlin points out that Iser himself is never completely free of value judgments,[61] and we may note that much the same is true for her. Even with her tolerance for what she feels are negative responses by Wayne Booth to *Come and Go*, we can still sense her search for a "correct" and "affirmative" solution—which of course clearly involves avoiding "an ethically-motivated approach."

However, Laughlin *is* able to do what Iser himself has yet to do—that is, to formulate and demonstrate an Iserian version of playreading. As noted earlier, Iser's own essay on Beckett is oriented toward the spectator rather than the reader. Throughout her essay, we never lose sight that Laughlin is basing her argument not on a viewing of *Come and Go* but on a reading, or to be more precise, on *her* reading. Thus, Laughlin succeeds in widening the concept of the reader's ability to imagine multiple and often opposing responses to a dramatic text; hers is an extremely useful contribution.

Nonetheless, as I mention at the beginning of this section, the most salient discussion of playreading in light of reader-response criticism remains Kirsten Nigro's 1987 essay, "On Reading and Responding to (Latin American) Playtexts." Here, the writer explicitly identifies the reader:

> [I]n this essay I am concerned with a particular species of "armchair" reader: the one in North American universities who, like me, reads and writes about twentieth-century Latin American drama. . . . So the reader I have in mind usually must imagine a play in performance based almost exclusively on the clues provided by the playtext.[62]

Reading other articles, like Booth's or Laughlin's, we may have assumed that the "reader" implied by the "we" was the author, or we may have accepted the inscribed or the implied reader. Here, the "we" is deliberately described.

Furthermore, rather than accepting, as do Booth and Laughlin, that the text "sets the limits of its possible readings,"[63] Nigro tries to counter the idea that the playscript is entirely literary in nature. She paraphrases Patrice Pavis's point that "the history of drama is not one so much of changing strategies of *writing*, as it is of changes in *play production* . . . ."[64] This statement has considerable impact:

This means that if it is acceptable to speak of reader competency, as so many reader-response theorists do, then in the case of drama this competency must include a familiarity with and understanding of conventions of performance and the strategies they employ in different theatrical modes and historical periods. Without some sense of how these conventions work it seems to me most difficult to discuss audience reaction, and it is certainly risky to assume that it operates in the exact same way that reader response to the printed word does.[65]

On the surface, this sounds strikingly similar to what Styan and other performance-oriented critics, including John Russell Brown, Theodore Shank, and Bernard Beckerman, have suggested; in fact, Nigro refers to them as "closet reader-response critics, in that one of their major concerns is with the way virtual or real performances are perceived by readers and audiences of theatregoers."[66] More profoundly, in terms of reader-response theory, Nigro's remarks imply that readers, whom she has already insisted must be identified, necessarily play a far greater role in "creating" the audience than they are said to by critics like Booth, Iser, and Laughlin, who look for the spectator inscribed in the text. (In this part of her essay, Nigro sounds very much like David Scanlan, whose search for an inscribed spectator relies, at least in part, on specific conventions of performance which directly involve the audience.)

"I should add as an aside here," Nigro interjects in a note,

that theatre practitioners are far more confident in their role as playtext readers; indeed, many of them might find it puzzling that 'reader-response' should even be an issue, since they always read with an eye to the audience.[67]

The confidence to which Nigro alludes is not quite as straightforward as it sounds. After all, inasmuch as directors, designers, and actors do read with a habitual "eye to the audience," they approach the text armed not only with "a familiarity with and understanding of conventions of performance and the strategies they employ" but also with a very specific (and *concrete*) notion of *who* the spectators are or at least have been. In a sense, such readers look both at the text of the play and to the "text" of the audience—the body of information which the readers themselves "write" (at least in their minds) regarding who is watching in the auditorium.

Nigro, however, does not follow up on this implication. Rather, she seems more interested in linking the theatre conventions inscribed in the text to audience responses. For example, her own reading of Udolfo Usigli's drama *El gesticulador*[68] focuses on the theatrical circumstances of stage realism in which audience members find themselves during a performance of this play as the leading influence on spectator response. This interest, of course, is consistent with her earlier statements based on Pavis.

Still, Nigro is not oblivious to the importance of knowledge of a real audience or real audiences. In fact, her essay builds to a recognition of the danger in our belief that "the signified were totally transcultural or free-floating," detecting in such a presumption an "imperialism, in that we impose our signification systems and values on others, regardless of cultural peculiarities."[69] She cites critic Juan Villegas, whom she compares to Hans Robert Jauss, on measures to correct reader "imperialism." In particular, she draws from Villegas the idea that readers, instead of considering "the hypothetical and/or individual reader," would do better to concentrate "on real readers [in this case, spectators] in a specific socio-cultural context."[70] In her own examination of Usigli's drama, she says, this would entail

> going far beyond the analysis proposed here; for example, to a consideration of Realism on the Mexican stage and of Usigli's own theories about it; to a discussion of the play's 1948 premiere, when both the political Left *and* Right felt alluded to; and, since theatre studies are not just archaeology, to an analysis of audiences seeing the play today, or perhaps better said, not seeing it today, since *El gesticulador* is rarely staged professionally in Mexico these days.[71]

This kind of analysis, Nigro suggests, would perhaps prove both very complex and extremely extensive.

Nigro ends by quoting Villegas on theatre research, emphasizing that he "speaks of 'una serie de estudios,' and not one, allembracing study." This emphasis is perhaps understandable given the scope of her own article. Nigro presents both a rigorous audience-oriented criticism of dramatic texts and an illuminating notion of what a reader-response theory of playreading might include. The length of her essay—nine pages, not including notes—makes her achievement all the more impressive.

Nigro's work, seen in the light of Booth's and Laughlin's, lends credence to the possibility that, even though reader-response critics have neglected the reading of playscripts, reader-response criticism is in fact capable of making significant contributions to the study of drama. However, before moving to a discussion of playreader constructs of audiences, we must confront one more topic that is inextricably linked to playreading: reader-response attitudes toward the *Poetics* of Aristotle. A good place to begin this discussion is with Mardi Valgamae's brief essay.

Reader-Response Criticism on Aristotle's "Poetics"

While examining the more traditional literature of playreading I have observed that the way in which writers discuss Aristotle indicates much about their own literary orientation. In turning now to reader-response depictions of the *Poetics,* we find more complicated instances of the same phenomenon. Most reader-response critics do have something to say about what is often, wrongly or rightly, regarded as the founding document of literary, dramatic, and even reception theory; yet, surprisingly, none of them say very much. Even so, I should add that there is a wide spectrum of opinion, from those who sincerely see Aristotle as the first reader-response critic to those who claim to view the *Poetics* as an ancient and thus a culturally alien tract.

Before illustrating these extremes, I wish to present an example of a more moderate position, one that is both more representative of what most of the reader-response literature implies and more attuned to dramatic texts. In "Drama as an Art Form: Four Critical Approaches," Mardi Valgamae looks at modern plays from the Baltic region. Valgamae, writing a dozen years after the publication of Booth's paper, spotlights what he calls (referring to M. H. Abrams's *The Mirror and the Lamp*) "four components of the world of aesthetics": "the universe, which art may imitate"; "the artist, whose subjective expression may define the work of art"; "the work itself"; and "the audience."[72] In his examination of each component, Valgamae employs what appear to be different literary theories: classical mimetic, romantic, structuralist, and reader-response. In fact, his readings of theory are probably more interesting than his readings of the specific plays.

Valgamae begins with Aristotle's mimetic theory. Although he agrees with Auerbach that "imitation as practiced by modern realists is not quite the same as the mimesis of the ancients,"[73] he feels justified in applying the principles of mimetic art to *Lazybones,* Hugo Raudsepp's 1932 Estonian comedy in which the hero is too lazy even to court a wife. This application leads to a discussion of dramatic form:

Raudsepp proceeds to a comic inversion worthy of Aristophanes. As did *Lysistrata,* which presents heterosexual antics that must have seemed droll to the homosexual audience of 5th-century B.C. Athens, Raudsepp's comedy capitalizes on inversion . . . . The phlegmatic protagonist of *Lazybones* is not gay. It is just that courting a girl requires the expenditure of an unseemly amount of energy.[74]

This shift in subject from imitation to structure and then to audience response is characteristic of Valgamae's tendency throughout. For example, later in his essay, while focusing on romantic theory (or, as he calls it, "expressive theory"), Valgamae offers an example involving Finnish playwright Hella Wuolijoki, whose dramatization of the life of Estonian poet Lydia Koidula caused much controversy.[75]

Finally, after using structuralism to explain structural relationships in Vaino Vahing's *Summerschool,* Valgamae brings reader-response theory directly into his discussion of possible audience reactions to an Estonian drama, Rein Saluri's *Who Am I?.* He proposes that Western European audiences would respond to the play differently from audiences in the Soviet Union, where the play was first produced.[76] Rather abruptly and unexpectedly, Valgamae ends his essay by generalizing about his varied approaches:

> All I am trying to suggest is that there are significant parallels between the contemporary reader-response theory and the mimetic tradition of the Greeks. Aristotle's concept of catharsis, after all, placed the effect of purgation in the spectator. Even Plato might agree that we have traveled [from mimetic to reader-response theory] what could be construed as a full circle.[77]

There is minimal preparation for this conclusion. Valgamae does not explain just what those "significant parallels" might be, nor does his essay clarify what "full circle" is supposed to mean—a 360 degree turn or perhaps a continuum. Nonetheless, the implications of this short article, which deals with plays that few English-speaking readers know, lead in a cryptic or perhaps merely informal manner toward a connection of some importance for many reader-response critics.

David Bleich in chapter four of *Subjective Criticism,* alludes to the *Poetics* as a work whose commentary on response has been distorted.

> In one sense, response has occupied this fundamental position for a long time. Aristotle, for example, defined tragedy as that sort of drama to which the audience's response is pity and fear, where such

feelings mark the evaluative identification of the dramatic experience. By similar reasoning, the mere description of a work as comic or of a character as pathetic shows how response defines what we perceive. But because of the paradigmatic imperative to keep the symbolic object objectively real, the ensuing critical discussion is always characterized by the respondents' arbitrary shifts from their own responses to the assumed factualities of the object.[78]

Bleich is criticizing readings of Aristotle by objectivist critics and is also claiming an affinity between his own reader-response position and that of Aristotle. This feeling, in fact, is one that he shares with a few other reader-response critics, such as Rosenblatt[79] and Holland.[80] They also link what we may think of as "Aristotelian reception theory" to their own concepts of literary response. "The Greeks," maintains Holland, in *5 Readers Reading* (1975), "observed the phenomena they ascribed to audiences better than later theorists . . . ."[81] In other words, Bleich, Rosenblatt, and Holland comprehend the *Poetics* within the framework of their own critical theorizing, which ironically, like the theoretical frameworks of the objectivists whom they contradict, helps them to see the ancient treatise in a way that conforms to their own views.

Tompkins, in her essay "The Reader in History," offers a view diametrically opposed to the one given by Bleich, whose fourth chapter of *Subjective Criticism* she in fact includes along with her own essay in *Reader-Response Criticism*. Tompkins says of Aristotle, "although he speaks of pity and fear as the emotions proper to tragedy, [he] judges the merit of poetic production in general on 'vividness of impression,' and 'concentrated effect' . . . ." She then concludes that "it is not the *nature* of the impact that concerns him, but the degree."[82] Tompkins is intent on supporting the thesis that all modern literary criticism shares the same premise ("to specify meaning")[83] and thus she dismisses the notion that reader-response theory bears any real similarity to the criticism of antiquity.

> In fact, despite initial appearances, the 'affective' criticism practiced by critics in the second half of the twentieth century owes nothing to the ancient rhetorical tradition it seems at first to resemble, and almost everything to the formalist doctrines it claims to have overturned.[84]

Interestingly, in *Sensational Designs* (1985), Tompkins uses Aristotle much as any objectivist critic would, mentioning his "canons of unity"[85] and his rules regarding plot.[86] Similarly, Stanley Fish, throughout "Structuralist Homiletics" (collected in *Is There a Text in This Class?*) refers to the *Poetics* as a discussion of literary structure.[87] True, it would be foolish to deny that Aristotle is concerned with how a work of literature is put together, but should reader-response critics deny altogether that the *Poetics,* and indeed other ancient critical works, contain the seeds of an audience-oriented theory of reading?

The answer, I believe, is no. Indeed, European reception theorists seem better prepared to locate themselves in the history of literary theory than their reader-response counterparts. I believe this is due, at least in part, to their ability to see the genealogy of reception theory as complex but profuse; for example, Peter Lebrecht Schmidt in "Reception Theory and Classical Scholarship: A Plea for Convergence" (1985),[88] points to earlier versions of reception theory both in classical literature and in nineteenth- and twentieth-century studies of the classics—a major component of the education of many, if not most, European critics. Thus, European critics are perhaps more knowledgeable and hence more realistic about the nature of their descent from Aristotle.

Hans Robert Jauss, in "Sketch of a Theory and History of Aesthetic Experience" (1967), says that in chapter 4 of the *Poetics,* "Aristotle corrected the 'straightline mechanism' on which Plato had based his condemnation of art," and identifies this as the most important point in the genesis of reception aesthetics.[89] Jauss examines too (and far more thoroughly than Tompkins) the sophist Gorgias, who "was interested in the 'preparation' of the listener of a speech and the transformation of his passionate interest into a new conviction which 'irresistibly forms his soul as it pleases'."[90] Jauss also points to St. Augustine's distinction between "the good use of sensual pleasures [notably, auditory] . . . and the bad."[91] Jauss's ability to discuss his own precursors appears more expansive and thus less reductive than either Bleich's or Tompkins's.

Moreover, as Holub summarizes it, Aristotle's legacy is mitigated and assisted by centuries of scholarship:

In the German tradition, Lessing's exegesis of Aristotelian categories is perhaps the best-known example of a theoretical departure in which the effect that a drama exerts on the individual viewer is accorded substantial emphasis. In a larger sense, however, the entire aesthetic tradition of the eighteenth century, from its beginnings as a separate branch of philosophical enquiry in Baumgarten's 1750 treatise *Aesthetica* to Kant's *Critique of Judgement* (1790), relies on notions of what the artwork does as much as what it is.[92]

Like Tompkins, Holub goes on to focus on more recent critical movements. Unlike Tompkins, Holub never finds it necessary to reject the venerable ancestry of reception theory. Both Tompkins and Holub are no doubt right in believing that the literary theory of the past century has been far more influential on the development of contemporary audience-oriented theory, at least in general. However, what makes the *Poetics* such an important source for this study, particularly in light of its principal concerns, is that Aristotle's main topic here is dramatic texts.

In the first section of this chapter I have offered reasons to explain why reader-response critics have avoided discussing the reading of dramatic texts; this in turn may, at least in part, explain why there is no serious reader-response discussion of the *Poetics*. However, there is yet another reason, I think, why reader-response critics tend to drop Aristotle's name but never actually use him: they have not read Aristotle in the original. Such an inference may be drawn not only from Tompkins's and Fish's reliance on the *Poetics* as a formalist guide but also from Rabinowitz's use of the word *imitation,* noted earlier in this chapter: "drama imitates the fictional event itself, while a narrative imitates an account of it . . . ." Rabinowitz's wording is clearly influenced by S. H. Butcher's translation of the *Poetics* (1894).[93]

Butcher, in what for decades remained one of the most respected versions of the *Poetics* in English, translates *mimēsis* as "imitates."[94] True, Butcher ultimately clarifies this translation later in his commentary:

> Art, therefore, in imitating the universal imitates the ideal; and we can now describe *a work of art as idealized representation of human life— of character, emotion, action—under forms manifest to sense.*
>
> "Imitation," in the sense in which Aristotle applies the word to poetry, is thus seen to be equivalent to 'producing' or 'creating according to a true idea,' which forms part of the definition of art in general.[95]

However, Stephen Halliwell, commenting on his own translation of the *Poetics* (1987), notes that

> "imitation" is now the least adequate (though still a regrettably common) translation of "mimesis." Our difficulties in understanding this concept arise in part from the fact that Ar. nowhere offers a definition of it; and this is one reason why my translation often leaves the term simply transliterated. Elsewhere, I usually favour the translation "representation" (or alternatively "portrayal"), because the English usage

of this word (and cognate forms) comes closest to the range of meanings covered by the mimesis word-group in Greek.[96]

And Richard Janko, in introducing his translation (1987), defines
mimēsis as follows:

> The Greeks drew no clear distinction between imitation, copying, im-
> personation, and representation—all these concepts were included in
> the word *mimēsis* .... Plato tends to stress the idea that visual art
> *copies* nature and Homer *impersonates* his characters; neither aspect of
> *mimēsis* is very complimentary to art. Aristotle redefines *mimēsis* to
> stress that poetry *represents* ideas. . . .[97]

Imitation is at best an unfortunate choice of words. Clearly, when
a twentieth-century reader-response critic, like Rabinowitz, takes
up the terminology of the nineteenth century, difficulties almost
inevitably arise.

If Halliwell is right in charging that Butcher's approach to the
Poetics constitutes "the final attempt of Romanticism in England
to appropriate some of Aristotle's views for its own cause,"[98] then
we may begin to understand why modern critics who rely on his
translation tend to come away with Butcher's reading of the *Poetics*.
In fact, Butcher himself, in commenting on the text, betrays his
own inability to reconcile Aristotle's ideas on reception with late
Victorian aesthetic thinking.

> To those who are familiar with modern modes of thinking it may
> seem a serious defect in the theory of Aristotle that he makes the end
> of art to reside in a pleasurable emotion, not in the realisation of a
> certain objective character that is necessary to the perfection of the
> work. . . . Aristotle's own definition too of art as "a faculty of produc-
> tion in accordance with a true idea," is quoted [from the *Nicomachean
> Ethics*, vi.4.1140a10] as showing that he was not far from assigning to
> fine art an end more consistent with his whole system. If art in general
> is the faculty of realising a true idea in external form, he might easily
> have arrived at a definition of fine art not essentially different from
> the modern conception of it as the revelation of the beautiful in exter-
> nal form.
>   It is probably not possible to acquit Aristotle of some inconsistency
> of treatment.[99]

Butcher is not entirely oblivious to what Aristotle is really saying
about the relationship between the audience and the work of art.
Rather, Butcher's own views on art compel him to neutralize and

even deny any implications that the *Poetics* contain a viable audience-oriented approach.

So Butcher goes on to recast audience response: "The subjective emotion is deeply grounded in human nature," he maintains, "and thence acquires a kind of objective validity."[100] Butcher asserts that Aristotle is referring not to just *any* audience but to "the judgement of a cultivated public."[101] And from such a public comes the proper "hedonistic effect," which "is not alien to the essence of the art, as has sometimes been thought; it is the subjective aspect of a real objective fact."[102] Thus, the work of art remains an objective reality which subjective response merely validates. With such a partisan distortion of the work, is it any wonder that American critics, from Brooks and Heilman (who abridge Butcher)[103] to Tompkins (whose few quotes from Aristotle in "The Reader in History" are also taken from Butcher)[104] have viewed the *Poetics* as a formalist guide?

In the context of reader-response criticism, at any rate, we may observe that in spite of persistent references to the *Poetics*, little has been written about it. References to the ancient philosopher have amounted to little more than academic name-dropping. Aristotle-as-founding-receptionist is an idea that American reader-response critics either embrace or reject, but the embrace is merely part of a flirtation and the rejection appears to be based on a rather superficial acquaintance.

Conclusion

Reader-response criticism has by and large failed to examine the reading of playscripts; its reluctance even to take note of this failure is an indication of how acute the failure is. The critical orientation of mainstream reader-response critics and their commitment to "reader-response theory" (if such may be said to exist) or to what Nigro characterizes as a reader-response posture are in part responsible for this failure. In addition, factors endemic to the role played by all critics in the academy, regardless of their theoretical orientation and affiliation, have contributed to the almost complete neglect of the playscript by reader-response critics; they maintain a tradition according to which literature includes only narrative fiction and poetry.

The few fringe reader-response essays available on reading playscripts suggest that it is certainly possible to discuss playreading in reader-response terms. These essays provide too a sense of the inadequacies of current reader-response approaches. The move from Booth's inscribed audience, which seems to respond in unison, to Laughlin's Iserian implied audience, which responds in various and possibly even contradictory ways, parallels the development of reader-response theories from a rather simple, monolithic rhetorical model to a more pluralistic reception model. Nigro's outline of a more complex critical study of audiences, extending beyond the text to audiences themselves, suggests several steps that critics may take beyond the "implied spectator."

Valgamae's claim that all critical theories inevitably relate back to Aristotelian reception and forward to reader-response criticism, vague though it may be, has led us to consider the *Poetics* as a reader-response document. Although European reception theorists have clearly traced their ideological ancestry back to Aristotle, reader-response critics have never adequately addressed what the ancient philosopher has written about audience response. We perhaps should not blame them for choosing the ancient discourse on tragedy as a precursor for their own writings; we ought, however, to question their reluctance to discuss the treatise. This questioning inevitably leads to considerations of the *Poetics* as a work that deals with the reader's involvement with the dramatic text and with the reader's consequent sense of the theatre audience.

4

The Reader and the Spectators

Introduction

According to the available literature, readers are aware of three distinct playreading dimensions. To get through most playscripts, readers create a sense of story—some narrative line that they can follow which resembles the plots they have experienced while reading fiction. They tend also to look closely at what is put into the mouths of characters, at the language of the speeches in the script, much as they would scrutinize the lines in a poem. In addition, to gain a clearer sense of the playscript as a play on stage, readers strive to give form in their imaginations to those stage-related parts of the playscript (such as set and character descriptions and stage directions) that are neither narratively fictive nor linguistically poetic.

Yet, as I have tried to emphasize (and as what has been written on playreading seems at least to imply), plays are not merely the literature of the *stage;* they are the literature of the *theatre,* and therefore, audience members, those participants who though necessary to any theatre performance cannot be readily located in the playscript, must be taken into account by the playreader. When playreading excludes the play's spectators and what they do during the play's performance, the reader's understanding of the playscript lacks a sense of the script's true embodiment as a play. If narrative, language, and staging represent three dimensions in the reading of a dramatic text, spectator response may be said to correspond to a fourth.

As we have seen, most critics, whether of the traditional or the reader-response variety, have some difficulty in dealing explicitly with the notion of the playreader constructing a sense of the theatre audience. Many, like Cleanth Brooks and Robert Heilman, cling to the playscript, from which the audience is conspicuously absent. Even a close playreading by Kenneth Thorpe Rowe, who

84

advocates that the reader construct a mental playhouse, leaves out that section of the building in which the audience sits.

Other writers, however, like Stephen Booth, Karen Laughlin, and David Scanlan, bring to playreading a more inventive view of what constitutes a play's text and detect, as chemists say, some trace amount of audience response in the playscript itself. Others still, such as Roger Gross and Kirsten Nigro, go so far as to admit that the playreader's job is in part to transcend the playscript, to construct, with the help of any clues included in the playscript and any relevant additional material outside the text, a notion of theatre audience response.

The writers reviewed in chapters 2 and 3 offer diverse glimpses of just who the playreader's audience may be. As indicated above, one way in which playreaders relate to the need for a sense of theatre spectators is through their creation of a *rhetorical* audience, the one to which Booth and others refer; the rhetorical house is often said to be implicit or inscribed in the text itself. There is also what Gross calls the *hypothetical* audience, a concept founded not merely upon information drawn from the text but from knowledge of that which is outside the playscript. Beyond this, there is an *actual* audience to which Nigro alludes, a construction or rather a reconstruction of the responses of those who actually came to see a performance of the play. Finally, built from all three, rhetorical, hypothetical, and actual audiences, is what I (basing my concept on a suggestion by Nigro) will call the *speculated* audience; the speculated house constitutes the playreader's attempt to invent an audience comprised of real people who never saw the play as produced or to invent a new production of the play for an actual or imagined audience.

This chapter defines these four playreader's audiences, exploring each. The exploration offered here proceeds on a general and for the most part an abstract level, referring back to the writers reviewed in the previous two chapters. In the chapter following, I illustrate these audience constructs more specifically and concretely through a series of readings of Jean Genet's *Les bonnes*.

The Rhetorical Audience

The usual rationale for (or defense of) the rhetorical audience is that it is based on information contained in the playscript. For example, the text of the play may include a sequence of actions, a series of dramatic images, or a set of conventions in which playreaders feel they find some description of the theatre audience. Upon such specific elements in the playscript, playreaders build what is supposed to be an objective sense of the responses of a play's spectators.

Of all the constructs offered in this study, the rhetorical audience seems, at least initially, the one most readily available to any playreader and also the one most relevant to the text of the play, for it is usually presented as being a logical extension of the text. Furthermore, because readers believe they derive the rhetorical audience from the script itself, they can and often do claim for this construct enormous authority, especially if they are in the process of considering the play (or rather, the playscript) as literature. All readers, we may at first believe, can easily widen their playreading to include the spectators' dimension by making use of this concept.

Yet there are serious shortcomings in depending on the rhetorical audience. For example, as noted earlier, in his pioneering essay on *Hamlet* Booth maintains that the play is "a succession of actions upon the understanding of an audience." His discussion of the audience's responses to the dead king's sudden entrance is premised on the idea that all the members of the house are reacting in unison. More disturbingly, intrinsic to Booth's methodology is the notion that the responses of his spectators are necessarily identical with those of the reader. The interruption by the ghost, Booth maintains, "both fulfills and frustrates *our* expectations: it is what *we* expect and desire, an action to account for *our* attention to sentinels"[1] (italics mine). Thus, although Booth's spectators are never explicitly identified, the playreader is almost imperceptibly equated, through Booth's use of the first person plural, with his rhetorical audience; in other words, the audience's response for Booth becomes identified with the reader's response.

At first Karen Laughlin appears to utilize the rhetorical audience very differently. Yet, while searching for "the role laid out for the reader by the text itself,"[2] she remarks that "many of the textual strategies of *Come and Go* are related to its orientation toward performance and should work to guide the responses of the armchair reader and the theatre spectator alike."[3] Thus, her ultimate conclusion, in spite of her ability to explain (as Booth cannot) *divergent* audience reactions, is weakened by the same problems that Booth encounters with *Hamlet*. Laughlin's rhetorical spectators are, like Booth's, nameless, faceless, nonspecific.

And once again, the "armchair reader and spectator" are united as respondents.

Scanlan's guide for student playreaders reveals the process through which the rhetorical audience is constructed. He too maintains that "[t]he reader can imagine the *responses* of an audience by noticing what kind of role they are given in the script"[4] and illustrates this by referring to such conventions as the fourth wall, the aside, and the chorus, all of which can be found in the playscript. Yet Scanlan advises that the reader use what Peter Shaffer calls "the communal imagination," adding that, though the reader can never know what an audience will do until a play is performed, "we can know how we as readers react, and we can extend our reactions to include what we know about the tastes, interests, and typical responses of our family, friends, and community."[5] In this way, Scanlan conveys that the rhetorical audience is the playreader's projection. That is to say, it is not so much an extension of the playscript as it is an extrapolation of the playreader and of the playreader's understanding of how people generally behave.

The dangers in such an approach are formidable. Scanlan's basic premise, that "[i]f we go to parties, attend performances or sports events, or spend time in classrooms, we already know a lot about the communal imagination,"[6] can easily result in what Nigro calls cultural "imperialism, in that we impose our signification system and values on others, regardless of cultural peculiarities."[7]

Consequently, playreaders who rely too heavily on the rhetorical audience run the risk of entrapping themselves in their own perceptions. While this reader construct of the theatre audience appears to be founded upon the text itself, readings built upon it are only as good as playreaders' abilities to be fair and objective in projecting themselves into the house and in equating reader responses with spectator responses. In this light, even Laughlin's explanation of differing responses in the same house becomes limited and problematic; after all, she can explain only those responses that she herself can imagine—which in large part clarifies her ambivalence over what she feels are Wayne Booth's qualms about Beckett.[8]

As recent books by Michael Gruber and Stanton Garner confirm, the faceless, nameless rhetorical audience persists in asserting its text-related authority. With regard to staking so much on so generalized an audience, Nigro, referring to Juan Villegas, proposes we concentrate "on real readers [or spectators] in a specific socio-cultural context."[9] True, readers may not always find it practical or even possible to try to reconstruct the actual, historical audience. Nonetheless, playreaders need to do more than filter themselves through the text and claim that their resultant, subjective sense of audience is an objective, text-oriented view. The next section, which looks at the hypothetical audience, proposes a construct both more realistic and more useful than the rhetorical audience.

The Hypothetical Audience

Like the rhetorical audience, the hypothetical audience is a projection by the playreader. However, the hypothetical projection, while it necessarily pertains to the playscript, is not (and does not pretend to be) an extension of the text itself. Rather, the hypothetical audience is based primarily on information which is not a part of the text and which is relevant to those circumstances—theatrical, historical, cultural, political, economic, or a combination of these and others—which involve the play's spectators.

The hypothetical audience is remarkably flexible: it may be located in the past, the present, even the future. At the same time, unlike the rhetorical audience, it is not entirely faceless and nameless. The strength of this audience construct rests on how much knowledge the playreader can bring to the reading.

As noted in chapter 2, Gross uses *hypothetical* in describing one of the two "audience levels" of meaning "experienced by a percipient of the play/script." For Gross, the hypothetical view is "what an interpreter believes an ideal audience would experience, a 'public' meaning" in contrast to the functional view, which is "what actual individuals *do* experience in particular exposures to the play/ script, a 'private' meaning which can never be fully known by an interpreter *or* by the person experiencing it."[10] Although Gross here seems to be discussing what I have defined as the rhetorical audience, the precise context for his comments helps to clarify what he means. Gross is primarily interested in helping budding directors learn to think about the potential audience when they read playscripts, and implicit in his remarks is the idea that theatre professionals do in some way *know* their audiences.

Nigro remarks that "theatre practitioners," in contrast to academics, "are more confident in their role as playtext readers; . . . they always read with an eye to the audience."[11] As I mentioned in chapter 3, such professional playreaders are able, due to their own experiences, to bring to their playreading a strong sense of the houses before whom they have performed. They are thus able to read the playscript with reference to an audience whom they have mentally constructed, based on specific circumstances, theatre-related and otherwise. Similarly, Gross's readers are asked to read playscripts for prospective performances by keeping in mind audiences whom they have known.

In other words, Gross is urging directors-in-training to hypothesize the future audience(s) of their own productions. For Gross, we should recall, the play "in itself, means nothing."[12] As an event, the performance of a play "*is merely a medium, not in itself of interest but only as a device for organizing, controlling, and communicating the real interest, and experience of feeling, potentially at many levels, from the purely sensuous to the intellectual*"[13] (italics in original). Therefore, in Gross's own terms, for playreaders to imagine the play without imagining an audience responding to it is tantamount to playreaders being unable to regard the play as meaningful. The spectators whom Gross's playreaders are asked to imagine, then, form the construct which I have defined above and which Gross himself has termed the hypothetical audience.

While the rhetorical audience is derived, at least in theory, from the text and may be said to "experience" the same responses as the reader, the hypothetical audience is created from information beyond the text, and the hypothetical audience's "responses" (that is, the responses the reader attributes to this construct) seem to be separate from the reader's. Playreaders do not have to identify with the responses of the hypothetical audience. In fact, readers may construct this audience in order to distinguish their own responses from those of some theatre audience.[14] Regarded in this way, playreading becomes a process in which the playreader begins to create mentally the dynamic interaction between house and stage. With the hypothetical audience in mind, the playreader may arrive at an interpretation of the play that makes use of, but does not necessarily coincide with, the imagined audience response; to a certain extent, then, the playreader ends up interpreting the audience's interpretation.

The hypothetical audience, projected from information drawn from outside the text, is of course highly dependent on the information upon which it is based. For example, a student may, while reading Euripides' *Electra,* try to hypothesize the original audience and its responses, but if the playreader's knowledge of classical Greece is vague or superficial, the construct becomes highly idiosyncratic or subjective, and the reading inevitably suffers. The imagined audience in this case turns out to be more a rhetorical construct, founded on the text and on the reader's sense of self (Scanlan's "communal imagination"), than a hypothetical audience. These imagined spectators might easily miss moments in the play which ancient Athenians would have keenly noted and savored, such as Electra's entrance, dressed in rags and carrying a jar on her shaven head, or the Messenger's insinuation that Orestes, in killing Aegisthus, has murdered a man who was acting as his (Orestes') host. Although (as Gross would have it) without an audience the play ceases to carry theatrical meaning, when readers read *with* a hypothetical audience that lacks relevance to what may be known, then readers virtually guarantee that their imagined audience's responses are merely a projection of their own.

The utilization of the hypothetical audience is extremely useful in reading the texts of plays about which we have minimal production and audience information. Like the ancient Greek theatre, the Elizabethan has bequeathed us an impressive body of playscripts but relatively little data on those who came to see them performed. Alfred Harbage, in *Shakespeare's Audience*,[15] puts together an educated and insightful guess. True, his version of Shakespeare's audience has been contested by Ann Jennalie Cook (in *The Privileged Playgoers of Shakespeare's London* [1981]),[16] and her version in turn has been the object of serious revision by Andrew Gurr (in *Playgoing in Shakespeare's London* [1987]).[17] Still, this ongoing debate reflects the serious efforts to explore the nature of Elizabethan audiences. Without substantive documentation of these spectators, the best that readers can do is to hypothesize about them, but this sort of projection potentially offers readers a better audience-oriented reading than the rhetorical.

Of course, to a degree, all hypothetical readings reflect the limitations and prejudices of our knowledge. Yet the great advantage of this construct over the rhetorical is that the hypothetical audience forces the reader to take a step away from the script. The playreader imaginatively translates the dramatic text into a theatre text but then must also think about the audience's responses—which deconstructionists might regard as an adjacent or a parallel text. Even if the reader ultimately decides to embrace the hypothetical audience's response, there has been at least some distancing, some feeling that the reader is separate from those whom he or she has imagined experiencing the play in the theatre. There is at least some recognition that by reading the playscript the reader has thought of the performance (as opposed to a re-hearsal) of a play.

It is usually easy to see that the hypothetical audience is separate from the reader. In the example above, a student attempts to construct the responses of an Athenian audience of the past. Similarly, Gross's director-in-training hypothesizes the spectators of a future production. When time is not an estranging factor, then place may differentiate the playreader from the hypothetical audience. For instance, the reader of a play which has not yet been produced in New York but is running in London may approach the script with an eye to those current British houses; the reader may wonder what spectators in the West End make of the play and from there proceed to construct a hypothetical audience of present-day Londoners and imagine their responses.

However, readers may also hypothesize from their own experiences as audience members—indeed, they may project hypothetical spectators based on their knowledge of themselves and others *as theatregoers*. If in fact a reader is creating a hypothetical construct from such information and not just projecting (as Scanlan asks them to do) rhetorically, then the playreader's audience remains separate from both script and reader. With any hypothetical audience, the playreader retains a sense of being the reader and of being apart from (rather than a part of) the house.

The exhilarating debate over who came to the Globe suggests that the same audience may be hypothesized in radically divergent ways. Clearly, the little data we have on Elizabethan spectators not only invites but requires interpretation. For those playscripts for which we do have a greater amount of audience information the playreader may begin to move away from the hypothetical audience and toward what I call the actual audience.

The Actual Audience

In sketching out how she might improve her own reading of Rodolfo Usigli's *El gesticulador*, Nigro indicates that she would start by extending her study of the playscript's audience-related conventions, especially what she refers to as stage realism, and then go on to explore Usigli's own theories on this convention. In the terminology I have proposed, Nigro would be moving away from the script (and the rhetorical audience) and toward the cultural theatre conventions (and the hypothetical audience). She would next go on to a discussion of the play's 1948 première, when both the political Left *and* Right felt alluded to; and, since theatre studies are not just archaeology, to an analysis of audiences seeing the play today, or perhaps better said, not seeing it today, since *El gesticulador* is rarely staged professionally in Mexico these days.[18]

Here Nigro is offering two alternatives to the vague, subjective rhetorical audience and the disputable hypothetical audience. First, she proposes an investigation of what I call the actual audience, those who actually came to a performance of the play. Second, she suggests something very different, a construct composed not of the spectators who actually saw or might today see *El gesticulador,* but of those who never will see the play, which I call the speculated audience. In this section I look at the actual audience; in the section following, I present the speculated audience.

Earlier, I noted how Gross, while discussing the audience levels of meaning, draws a distinction between the hypothetical and functional views. The latter reflects "what actual individuals *do* experience in particular exposures to the play/script, a 'private' meaning which can never be fully known by an interpreter *or* by the person experiencing it."[19] For Gross, then, the functional audience's responses are difficult to know and thus difficult to work with. But does this mean that the functional or actual audience is entirely unknowable? And, if it is not, ought it to be avoided completely, even if we ultimately can know only a little of what there is to know?

An actual audience may, at least in part, be reconstructed through research. The reader's notion of the actual audience is based on specific, concrete information documenting genuine audience responses to an actual performance of a play—information which is necessarily drawn from sources outside the playscript. The reason for trying to identify specific audience responses from another time or place is not motivated by a desire to find the "true" or "correct" meaning of a play.

In fact, the preoccupation with determining the meaning of a work, which motivates much or most of (though not, as Tompkins in "The Reader in History" would have it, all) modern criticism, often subverts the possibility of seeing as equally valid responses that differ from each other in major ways. The contrast between the inmate audience's enthusiastic response to the 1957 San Quentin production of *Waiting for Godot* and the spectators' and critics' puzzled reception of the play's commercial debuts provides a good example of how actual responses may differ. Here one may draw on actual response in order to understand a playscript that playreaders otherwise may find meaningless.[20] Esslin's use in *The Theatre of the Absurd* of the responses of the actual San Quentin audience suggests that looking at the very different audiences and their responses may productively contribute to the process through which readers come to form their own responses. Learning how others have received the play may, in turn, lead the reader not to an identification of one meaning or more as correct but rather to an understanding of how to locate his or her own ideas of meaning with respect to other interpreters of the play (previous spectators and readers).

At the same time, examining and analyzing the real responses of real spectators can act as a useful corrective to those structuralist and poststructuralist approaches which avoid looking at *what* a play means and offer instead a view of *how* it signifies. Certainly, any information on what spectators *do* in the theatre is necessary to the study of a play. Some would deny that response in itself has any meaning. They would insist, for example, that a divided crowd actively arguing during the intermission and carrying on the debate long after the curtain has fallen, as was the case for the first audiences of Edward Bond's *Saved*, does not offer us some notion of what (as well as how) the play signifies. But this would be to defer indefinitely the act of interpretation through which meaning is assigned. That such acts are transitory and limited is a fact which even the eternal deferral of interpretation cannot change.

Although readers may find it difficult to locate information on specific audiences and their actual responses, materials do exist. Theatre reviews and notices, memoirs, diaries, and letters, and other written sources such as account books, may provide a glimpse of actual spectators. Of course, in contrast to the amount of documentation available on specific productions, there may seem to be comparatively little evidence from which to build a clear sense of who responded to a particular performance of a particular play—and of how they responded to it.

The importance of the hypothetical and actual constructs becomes particularly apparent when we recall how critics justify their use of the rhetorical house. Stanton Garner, whose theoretical discussion of audience response is complex and sophisticated, turns Gross's hypothetical audience into what I call the rhetorical. Garner makes his imagined spectators

> a representative audience in order to suggest the mental parameters
> with which dramatic narrative achieves its cognitive manipulations. . . .

> Variables of history and culture are necessarily minimized [in this
> study], but they are by no means precluded by this study's stress on
> the more immediately cognitive dimensions of response. . . .[21]

This argument rests on the critic's belief that a work of dramatic
literature's "cognitive dimensions of response" may be examined
without reference to the "[v]ariables of history and culture" and
that all theatre audiences, regardless of when and where and how
they have lived, fall within the same "mental parameters"—that
is, they basically respond in the same way. This "representative
audience," guided by the dramatic narrative's "cognitive manipu-
lations," is clearly neither Gross's hypothetical nor functional
views. Garner's construct here is obviously based on a rhetorical
model.

The hypothetical and actual constructs represent playreaders'
attempts to imagine theatre audiences more specific and more
real than those allowed through the rhetorical construct. Because,
as Nigro suggests, a play is not understandable outside a specific
"socio-cultural context,"[22] it is crucial to try to assemble (or rather
to reassemble), in spite of a scarcity of hard data, those who actually filled the auditorium and who, as Gross would put it, responded meaningfully.

The Speculated Audience

The speculated audience is initiated by pure conjecture.

Given our knowledge of ancient Athens, how would an audience comprised entirely of slaves have responded to Euripides'
Orestes, in which an actor depicting a slave delivers a disturbing
monologue about the plight of a slave? Or what would veteran
theatregoers in the late 1830s have made of a performance of
Dantons Tod (which was not produced until 1902)? Or what would
the house at the premiere of *The Emperor Jones* have done if the
title role had been played not by a black actor, but by a white actor
in blackface? Answers to such questions proceed from speculation; nonetheless, in order to answer them, the reader must engage in some of the same activities needed to construct the
rhetorical, hypothetical, and actual audiences.

The sort of close reading needed to construct the rhetorical
audience is required to construct the speculated audience, but
with a major discrepancy: the playreader is now armed with a
totally new and unorthodox set of givens—different house, differ-

ent production, different time in history—and thus must come back to the playscript with radically altered assumptions. When the playreader returns to *Waiting for Godot* but imagines an all-female cast on stage, even the responses of one's own, very personally projected spectators have to change. Speculation makes the rhetorical house more specific because one's speculations themselves begin to specify the house.

To an important degree, the speculated audience is similar to the hypothetical. But unlike the speculated audience, the hypothetical audience is usually a projection of the status quo. For example, those who write on Elizabethan audiences are usually striving to describe a *typical* group of spectators who by and large conform to what scholars know about late sixteenth-century society and culture; such critics are attempting to characterize what might have been the "normal" playhouse crowd. The speculated audience, however, is predicated on conditions that never occurred, conditions which in retrospect seem in some way abnormal, countercultural. It is somehow in opposition to current notions of the past that are in fact rooted in notions about the present—notions which we tend not to question. Rather than think about how the usual (hypothetical) house at the Globe responded to *Lear*, we might postulate how they would have received the kind of fare reserved for aristocrats, such as Jonson's *Masque of Blackness*.

The research required to construct the actual audience may be the starting point for the speculated. The reader may invoke the speculated audience as some sort of test against which the behavior of the actual house may be measured.

Thus, developing a speculated audience may allow us to think of responses that conventional approaches either make invisible or nullify. Making use of factual information to create a sense of one or more actual audiences may show us responses that differ quite radically from our own. In this way, the playreader must be prepared for the possibility of encountering a variety of meanings, all of which may in context be valid.

Conclusion

The rhetorical, hypothetical, actual, and speculated audiences represent for playreaders four possible conceptualizations of spectators. The important point here, perhaps, is not that *one* construct is necessarily better than another. In effect, playreaders may draw upon one, two, three, or upon all four, depending on why they are reading a playscript. Consequently, a clear understanding of what each construct is and what it represents is needed.

In this chapter, my discussion has been abstract. Although I have tried to illustrate my ideas with short examples, the notion of audience constructs may not appear meaningful without a more developed application to a particular playscript. For this reason, the next chapter examines each of the respective playreader audiences for four separate but related readings of *Les bonnes* by Jean Genet.

5

Playreader Audiences for Genet's *Les Bonnes*

Introduction

Throughout this study I have maintained that an understanding of a playscript—of *any* playscript—requires a reading which takes into account not merely its fictive and poetic elements and its production possibilities, but also the role played during the play's performance by the theatre audience. Having discussed on an abstract level four playreader constructs of theatre audiences, I now turn to the reading of a particular playscript and to a demonstration of the ideas offered in the previous chapter. The specific playscript I have chosen is Jean Genet's *Les bonnes,* known in English as *The Maids.*[1]

There are several reasons for my choice of *Les bonnes.* It is a relatively short though highly complex play and thus advantageously compact for this discussion; it has an interesting history of audience reception; and it is probably the most widely read and performed of Genet's plays, making it of intrinsic interest and significance. Still, while all these are no doubt valid reasons for my use of this play, my motives for choosing it are not all coldly rational. The fact is, I continue to think about *Les Bonnes,* I am fascinated by its production history and by how audiences have received it, and I feel I have something original to say about it.

In any case, I do believe that the problems encountered in a reading of *Les bonnes* may be viewed as representative of general problems in reading playscripts.

Before examining possible playreader audiences for *Les bonnes,* it is necessary to look at those other reading activities that must go on before the creation of playreader audiences can occur. These include constructing a fictive narrative, developing a sense of language, and creating an imaginary production of the play on stage. These are what I have earlier called the "three dimensions" of playreading; the playreader's audience forms the fourth. To emphasize that this initial discussion is not just about how *I* read dramatic texts but about how people in general respond to them, I will try in the next section to draw not only from my own responses but from the responses of others.

Reading "Les bonnes" in Three Dimensions

Readers who come to the playscript of Jean Genet's *Les bonnes* must engage in a number of playreading activities. Primary perhaps among these is their creation within themselves of a sense of a fictive event or of fictive events occurring. Although playreaders usually have a notion of things happening, what is significantly absent from a playscript is the apparently explicit narrative voice which they encounter in most narrative fiction. It is perhaps inevitable that most readers, most of the time, at least on some level do read playscripts in a narrative mode.

In this mode readers mentally translate the dramatic text into a sequence of fictive actions that occur in a fictive world; readers feel that they "encounter" a "story." It is a story which in fact they themselves construct, based on the playscript's dialogue and stage directions, and which they follow much as they would "follow" the story which they construct while reading a more explicitly narrated fictive text, such as a novel. In this mode, though, the *play* within the playscript appears to fade into the background, and the plot—that sequence of things happening—emerges clearly, almost independent of the stage-bound dramatic text.

Constructing a sense of narrative, of course, is not only basic to playreading but to the reading of virtually all fiction—so basic, in fact, that it has become conventional in discussing such literature to provide, usually for purposes of orientation, a synopsis of the action. Thus, in discussing *Les bonnes,* I owe the reader a précis of "what happens" in the play. I would like to utilize this convention to examine, if only briefly, the construction of narrative summary. To do this, I present three plot constructs which different individuals have believed they encountered in the dramatic text.[2] The first is short:

Two little maids, two sisters, in the bedchamber of their absent mistress, stir up their spite and intoxicate themselves with their misery, spewing up their "human condition"—and with such redundancy, such inspired style, oratory, hallucinatory! Quickly they choose up sides. They have sent an anonymous denunciation; they try to poison their mistress. . . . Knowing what is going to become of them and feeling utterly lost, one of the two drinks the poison. Thus the scorpion encircled by fire stings itself . . .

The second, despite an initial promise to be brief, offers more information, some of which may conflict with other readers' constructs:

> I won't enter into detail. Know only that Claire and Solange, who are sisters, in the absence of Madame, "play out" their hatred, in spite of their admiration, for her: one of them, then, is Madame, the other remains herself; the false Madame brutalizes her sister, insults her, and in what a fashion! The other shows herself at first as submissive, then bursts into invective, throws herself on her and appears to strangle her. Then the alarm clock goes off: it is the time when the real Madame is going to come home and when the game stops. This isn't all. One of the two maids has denounced Madame's lover to the police, and he has been incarcerated for theft. But the maids learn through a phone call that he is temporarily free; he will make an inquiry to know who has denounced him and will find out. . . . How to exorcise this menace? In the end, one of the maids consumes the poisoned tea that she prepared to eliminate Madame and which she has not had the courage to make her ingest.

The third account appears to spend more time and effort on defining a general and a specific sequence of events:

> [T]he maids are two sisters, Claire and Solange, who, dominated by their servile condition and intoxicated by humiliation, exorcise themselves through the "ceremony" that will transfigure them. The play traces the sad quest for authenticity, lived until death, of these two reprobates: fascinated by Madame, in an atmosphere of cloying sensuality, they have no autonomous existence; their material dependence is accompanied by a fanatical adoration, the other face of which is a terrible hatred. They exist only as a function of Madame: they serve her with love, surround her with childish attentions, and when she is not there, dream of her, imagine her, wait upon her, imitate her too; and that is precisely what they themselves call, in the language of initiates, the "ceremony": a black mass in which Claire plays Madame, while her sister is, for the moment, "the maids"; then, in minute doses, they respond to all the insults with contempt. This liking for acting, no doubt, and also for sacrilege, which is accomplished by reaching their game's end, might liberate them. But they never have time to

achieve their end: the hour strikes, their exaltation breaks into agony, Madame returns, and the obsession with the mundane takes over the normal course. But one day the maids want to break the charmed circle that seems to protect Madame and to place her and all that touches her beyond their reach; and it is Madame's lover whom they attack; with a letter of denunciation, Monsieur is arrested. Yes, but the spell goes against the maids, . . . and Monsieur is freed. They fail at their cwn liberation, are complete failures because Madame has not drunk the poisoned tea which they have prepared for her.

Thus the turning point is reached: this time, born out of spontaneity, the ceremony is completed; all rancor is exhaled, all judgments over past injuries are unrolled, and, to finish up, Solange-the-maid symbolically strangles Claire-Madame. Now they are delivered, but the deliverance will not be effective so long as the symbol remains incarnate; and Claire, with the dreadful lucidity of one in a dream, commands Solange toward the definitive acts which will give them each her liberty: death for one, crime for the other.

There are certain similarities and some obvious differences among these accounts. It is possible to discern in each some evidence of interpretation (and, with the second, of what seems to be misinterpretation with regard to whom Solange is playing when Claire plays Madame) and of evaluation, either negative (as with the first and second) or positive (as in the third). For all three, however, the narrative summary is for the most part fixed on the fictive events in the play rather than on any other aspect of the dramatic or theatre text.[3]

Still, there are points in the first two extracts where the writer fleetingly refers not to what happens but to the nature of the language used by characters. The two maids, says the first writer, complain about their fates "with such redundancy, such inspired style, oratory, hallucinatory!" In the game they play, says the second writer, "the false Madame brutalizes her sister, insults her, and in what a fashion!" Such observations are not entirely relevant to narrative; they are made as a result of those activities in which readers often engage while reading poetry.

A series of even more pointed descriptions of the words spoken by characters in the play shows not only that individual perceptions vary tremendously, but that constructing a sense of the play's language is also part of what many tend to do.[4] The following description declares that the dialogue has much in common with poetry:

[T]he language that Jean Genet has his domestics speak is very far from realism, and requires in some part a poetic transposition which the public hardly understands reaches toward a more profound truth.

A second description suggests something quite different about the language in the play:

> [T]he style of the play is one of inconceivable grandiloquence, and is fittingly what our fathers would have called a *"galimatias"* [a tangled and confused piece of writing], or better yet an *"amphigouri"* [a written piece impossible to follow and unintelligible]—these verbal messes whose maiden-name is the Saint-Ouen diarrhea from those times when the King's players forbade all others from uttering intelligible dialogue.

This third description takes yet another position on *Les bonnes:*

> It is written in a language sometimes a little too highly charged, and about which, in order to recapture a sense of the play, one hardly knows for certain if some of the expressions are spit or diamonds. But it is also a language of real power. . . .

In each of these, the writer regards the play not just as some fictive narrative but as a fabric of words, what we commonly call a text; and its language can and ought to be scrutinized with special care.

Whether the writer approves of Genet's style (as in the first extract), holds it in contempt (as in the second), or is impressed but ambivalent (as in the third), each writer is aware of a level of meaning separate from and beyond narrative. The ability of readers, then, to view the dramatic text as something more or something other than a narrative allows them to read playscripts in a way similar to that in which they would read a poem and to think of plays as potentially full of linguistic significance.[5]

Likewise, playreaders are able to grasp at the *play* implied by the playscript only when they begin to visualize imaginatively the "action" on a stage. Thus, playreaders who "see" *Hedda Gabler* taking place in the sitting room of a villa in a Norwegian city, rather than in a setting *made* to look in some way like such a room in such a locale, are in effect novelizing the play. Only when playreaders can distinguish the story action (Hedda in her dressing gown coming into the middle of her sitting room and looking depressed and tired) from the stage action (the costumed actress who is playing Hedda entering left, crossing the sitting room set to stage center), only when they can be aware of the simultaneous existence of both, can they understand how the dramatic text and the theatre text connect.

The "stage-centred reforms" to which J. L. Styan refers,[6] through which playreaders are encouraged to be aware of the play in performance, are vital in that they promote a kind of transcendence, away from the script as pure literature and toward the playscript as a work of the stage. For a play like *Les bonnes*, readers' conceptualizations of a theatre text are particularly useful because they may alter, often quite radically and meaningfully, readers' responses to the dramatic text.

Indeed, readers continue to come to the playscript of *Les bonnes* with wildly variant notions of what the play is like on stage. Sartre, invoking Genet as author and hence authoritative reader, envisioned the roles as played by three adolescent males; their performances would closely imitate those of female actresses, and they would be on a stage flanked by placards which would constantly remind the audience that the performers were not women.[7] Contrary to Sartre, when The Living Theatre first prepared to do the play (in 1965), Julian Beck and Judith Malina as playreaders saw the actors not as boys but as very masculine, well-developed men, and this utterly negated the ambiguity that necessitated placards. In spite of these two influential readings, many playreaders, from secondary students to theatre professionals, including the play's first director, Louis Jouvet and the director who (more than two decades after the play's debut) received Genet's approval, Victor Garcia, tend to imagine *Les bonnes* with female performers. Some readers think of realistic stage settings, while others reading the playscript see suggestive scenery under stark lighting.

The point here, of course, is not that there ever is or ought to be a single or correct way for playreaders to "view" a play, especially a play like *Les bonnes*. The point is, rather, that one clear advantage which playreading holds over theatregoing is that for playreaders there always remains the possibility that the style or form of the mentally "staged" play may easily alter and that several different stagings can take place concurrently.[8] Although readers may find it necessary to critique and revise their imagined productions and although we may judge some playreader productions to be better than others, what is crucial is that readers of playscripts benefit from constructing in their minds the play on stage.

Having put together a narrative, created a sense of language, and envisioned the play in production, many readers feel they have completed the process of playreading. Still, one more activity remains: constructing an audience. The first audience that play-readers may try to construct is the rhetorical.

The Audience "in" "Les bonnes"

The rhetorical audience, that construct based on information in the playscript itself, is perhaps the most challenging to locate with respect to *Les bonnes*. As I have noted in chapter 4, the great danger in this construct is that readers tend to use it subjec-tively. They project an audience into those places in the text of the playscript[9] where they sense an audience would respond. But pronouncements which claim to characterize the way that audi-ences—in effect, *all* audiences—of a play will react usually say more about a particular *reader's* concerns than about those of any specific audience or even about those of audiences in general.

Consequently, statements, such as the following by Jeannette Savona, immediately seem too broad if not extremely suspect:

> In *The Maids*, the spectator is expected to recognize himself in the remote "goodness" of both Madame and Monsieur, but he is more likely to become trapped in the maze of Claire's and Solange's fanta-sies and desires and thus to experience the confusion of their strange sexual feelings.[10]

I am not denying that Savona's rhetorical reading of the playscript here is a viable one, nor do I dispute that a particular house at a particular production of *Les bonnes* may respond as she predicts or prescribes. I do, however, question whether all audiences of all productions would do with the play what she says they would. I am, in fact, reasserting my earlier point that those who allege that they can describe the "effects" of the dramatic text without reference to any specific audience(s) are, for the most part, filling the seats of their mental playhouses with duplicates of themselves.

How, then, can readers use the rhetorical construct without jumping to conclusions? By doing the initial work of construction but refraining from that swift rush to judgment in which too many critics indulge. To locate in the playscript conventions that appear to implicate or engage an audience (an aside, the utiliza-tion of the fourth wall, the presence of a chorus) is not the same as supplying how audiences would respond to them.

Another way readers may benefit from the rhetorical construct requires them to accept that they, during some phase of the playreading process, are peopling the threatre with imagined clones of themselves and are thereby constructing an admittedly highly subjective and homogeneous theatre audience. To look for those places in the playscript where readers feel that they (if they themselves were in the house) would have some palpable response can thus serve as a starting point for readers to consider how their own personal responses compare with the responses of either a hypothetical or an actual audience. Clearly, playreaders need to resist the temptation to mistake what they themselves believe are legitimate responses for the responses of theatre audiences.

With these caveats in mind, I turn to *Les bonnes* and to a discussion of three elements in the playscript that seem to me to point, at least in terms of the rhetorical audience, toward spectator response: direct mention of the audience in the stage directions and indirect allusion in the dialogue to the audience; the presence of characters on the stage who are themselves performing; and the literal and figurative uses of (and the explicit and implicit references to) mirrors and mirroring.

Some readers may disagree with my selection of these three elements—in fact they are welcome to, for even though I genuinely feel that I have chosen what in the playscript most clearly pertains to the construction of a rhetorical audience, my premise remains that this process is extremely subjective and hence inevitably disputable. I hope that the ensuing discussion of these elements will convince other readers that my emphasis is reasonable, though certainly not definitive.

Earlier, I indicated that the rhetorical audience for *Les bonnes* was perhaps the most challenging construct to locate—or, to be more accurate, to build. Unlike some of Genet's later plays, *Les bonnes* does not remodel the stage and house to include the spectators. The actual mirrors on stage during this play, unlike those brought on throughout *Le balcon*, are turned not on the audience but on the stage players. Nor in *Les bonnes* are there, as in *Les nègres*, special directions for how ushers should seat audience members to whom the actors should direct their lines; nor is the house here, as in *Les paravents*, designated a separate realm.

Instead, *Les bonnes*, like *Haute surveillance*, appears to be written for a traditional theatre. True, Genet's subsequent remarks about how the play ought to be produced challenge my contention.[11] Nonetheless, in its published forms the dramatic text of *Les bonnes* seems to require a conventional twentieth-century French or realistic staging. Indeed, its author's two vehement protestations to the contrary (which have even been appended to French editions of the playscript) only underscore his views that performances of the play should transcend or even disregard much of what playreaders clearly discern in its script.

Direct reference to the audience (in French, *la public*) in the stage directions first occurs during Solange's long monologue toward the end of the play. After stepping onto the balcony, she delivers a long tirade "with her back to the audience" (EG 107, GP 93). After she has concluded and come back into the room, her sister enters. We learn that "visible only to the audience, CLAIRE, during the last few moments, has been leaning with her elbows against the jamb of the kitchen door and listening to her sister" (EG 109, GP 95). Then, at the very end of the play, as Claire drinks the cup of poisoned tea, Solange turns to face the audience (EG 113, GP 99).[12]

What can readers conclude from these references to *la public* which occur rather late in the play? On one level, readers may see a progression. The audience first feels snubbed by Solange, who turns her back to it while she is delivering what amounts to her grand aria. It then feels privileged to see Claire's entrance when Solange (who has already turned her back on the house) is not yet aware of it. Finally, it feels trapped in a confrontation with Solange, who for the first and only time in the play confronts the house directly. This, at least, is the sequence of responses which the audience I have in mind experiences.

Of course, the spectators I have in mind have, by the end of the play, inferred a connection between themselves and "the people opposite" *(les gens d'en face)*. These people ostensibly reside in the house across the way from Madame's, and are, the maids fear, watching what they have been doing (EG 35, 101; GP 48); they are possibly the ones who (in the 1954 version) Claire suspects are spying on them (GP 83). On their side, these spectators identify with the spies of the maids' paranoia, because they are keenly aware that for all the looking and listening discussed on stage, the real voyeurs and eavesdroppers are those seated in the auditorium. Therefore, Solange turning her back is especially troublesome for my audience, for the gesture appears to negate their earlier identification; likewise, her final direct appeal to the audience suddenly brings my spectators back into the play: they are, after all, quite suddenly implicated, much as accomplices are implicated in a crime, in what they have witnessed on stage.

My spectators' strong identification with the maids' paranoid constructs of people looking at them and listening to them derives from their consciousness that the actors are playing characters who are themselves performing. The audience I have in mind repeatedly encounters moments in which Claire's performance as Madame and Solange's performance as Claire are nothing more than performances. Disturbingly, at one point Madame's portrayal of Madame suggests that Claire's insipid characterization of her mistress is more the result of Madame's insipidity than of Claire's. It is almost as if these spectators, reflecting the attention which the actors are drawing to their roles as actors, become overly aware of their own roles as spectators. In this sense, the audience's self-consciousness mirrors the performers': true to the dynamics of the mirror, activities in the house form a faithful though noticeably inverted reflection of those on stage.

The mirror, as is obvious to my spectators, plays a central and an ongoing role in *Les bonnes*. The dressing table and its mirror remain on stage throughout. Claire as Madame primps before it (EG 18, GP 37); Madame talks to herself in front of it (GP 75); and in it she catches Claire entering on tiptoe with the poisoned tea (GP 76).[13] During their "game," Claire demands that Solange use Madame's patent leather shoes as a mirror (GP 37), and later Solange gives Claire a hand mirror (EG 30, GP 45).

Beyond this, the characters serve as mirrors for each other. Madame advises Claire on her makeup (EG 84, GP 73–74) and in turn asks Claire her opinion of her coiffure (GP 77), while Claire asks Solange if her rouge is excessive (GP 82). Mirrors make their way into the dialogue too: Solange alleges that Claire promenades about the apartment at night "looking at herself in the mirrors" (EG 39, GP 51); later Claire says of her sister, "I'm sick of seeing my image thrown back at me by a mirror, like a bad smell" (EG 58, GP 61). Finally, Claire and Solange not only mirror each other and Madame, but, as noted above Madame mirrors her maids' inverted image of herself (EG 68, GP 67).

What does this audience make of all these literal and figurative mirrorings? The spectators I have in mind do not merely take their cue from the actors playing actors and thus become spectators playing spectators, but more important they cease to regard what is framed by the proscenium as an operative looking glass. The whole concept of stage-as-mirror, according to which what is enacted on stage reflects what happens in life, they feel obliged to debunk, to negate. My audience ceases to regard the play itself as realistic and gradually comes to grapple with a piece of theatre that appears to be more than representational. The spectators in my imagined house understand that theatre, as a glass, distorts as it reflects: the truth is mirrored but it does not look as one expects or hopes it would.

If by now readers have tired of such phrases as "the spectators I have in mind" and "my audience," I am pleased to dispense with them entirely. I've purposely been overusing them to emphasize the rhetoricity of the construct.

Are the responses I ascribe to "my" audience typical of those that other audiences or audiences in general would exhibit at a performance of *Les bonnes?* At this point, even before I have begun to construct a hypothetical or an actual audience, I concede that they probably are not. This audience, which I have put together in order to exemplify a possible rhetorical construct based on *Les bonnes,* is comprised of many versions of myself. I have certainly no wish to argue that my responses, projected into an audience's, are typical of those of audiences in general, if only because I do not think they are. I know from experience that my own responses as a spectator tend to be rather idiosyncratic, even sometimes strangely inappropriate; yet they are my own and I think they are interesting. It is not that they do not deserve to be aired but that they do not deserve to be put forward as anything more (or, for that matter, anything less) than my subjective and personal reactions to the play.

At its best, the rhetorical audience indicates what readers regard as prominent loci of spectator activity—those places in a playscript where playreaders imagine an audience responding significantly to a performance of the play built upon the playscript. To be sure, the most interesting question remains, "*How* does the audience respond?" This is too often answered without any thought given to the question, "*Who* is the audience?" A clear danger remains in the way playreaders impose their own personal responses on their imagined audiences. This imposition is based on the idea (either directly stated or tacitly assumed) that all audiences essentially respond the same way. The major value in the rhetorical construct, perhaps, is that playreaders begin, through close reading, to accept that audience response to plays is an inescapable factor in any interpretation of dramatic literature.

Hypothesizing an Audience

As I have noted in chapter 4, the hypothetical audience, like the rhetorical, is projected by readers. Nonetheless, in creating

this construct, playreaders cannot justify their projections by citing the authority of "the text itself," nor should they claim their
own responses are the same as the imagined audience's. Instead,
playreaders base their hypothetical projections on information
that is largely extrinsic to the playscript so that they may imagine
spectators who are in some significant way different from themselves. The extratextual information that readers utilize may be
theatrical, historical, cultural, political, economic—anything which
allows them to formulate the responses of an audience in some
specific situation, some particular time or place or circumstance.

Because playreaders do not have to identify with the responses
of the hypothetical audience, their use of this construct turns
playreading into a process in which they can attempt to create or
recreate mentally the dynamic interaction between house and
stage. This attempt is, at least potentially, extremely positive in
that it may help readers circumvent the excessively subjective and
inappropriate interpretations at which they may be prone to
arrive.

For example, college students already skilled at reading playscripts as narrative and poetry and who can imagine a production
of *Measure for Measure* may still, due to their own limitations, impose upon the play a thoroughly incongruous meaning. For such
readers, the use of the rhetorical audience only further supports
their most unfortunate claims. The hypothetical audience, however, allows for the possibility of their observing, from some distance, the whole *play* in action—not just the play happening on
stage but the play as it is received in the house as well. Rather
than immediately assuming that the audience responds just as
they themselves do, these readers may consider those things that
make the hypothetical audience's responses unique and thus unlike their own. True, these students' interpretations of *Measure for
Measure* may, as a result of hypothesizing, be corrupted by various
misconceptions—by erroneous information, for example, on what
Elizabethan audiences thought about sex, theatre, and politics.
However, the informational errors which lead to a misinterpretation of the responses of the hypothetical audience may be discussed and corrected in some rational manner.

As I have asserted in the previous chapter, a hypothetical audience is only as good as the information upon which it has been
based. We may, for instance, maintain that a shock went through
the auditorium when the first spectators of Euripides' *Electra* saw
the title character enter in rags and carrying a water jar on her
shaven head. Although all the information we have, what little

there is, supports this supposition, we may yet uncover additional data, either specific (about how the actual audience laughed at Electra's entrance) or general (about how during the Peloponnesian War Athenian outrage at the portrayal of poverty waned), which may lead us to alter our hypothesis. Yet the hypothesis behind the construct may be adjusted, and the hypothetical audience and its responses, instead of being thrown out entirely, may be regarded in a new way.

By way of example, I am going to hypothesize some of the responses of the audience at the debut of *Les bonnes*. (The play opened in Paris in the spring of 1947 and had a relatively short, reportedly unsuccessful run.) I will base my hypothetical construct first on spectators' responses to the play's use of the case of the Papin sisters, the real-life murderesses upon whom Claire and Solange are based, and second on spectators' responses to the theatrical circumstances under which the play was originally mounted. I acknowledge that there are a number of other areas into which I might profitably go, such as the political upheavals shaking France when the play first opened or the changing intellectual climate; indeed, there are many possibilities, and to some degree, my choice of information upon which to construct my hypothetical audience reveals some of my personal interests.

Nevertheless, my purpose here is to illustrate the hypothetical audience, and although I have chosen to use information that I believe is in itself important, I also wish to demonstrate both a successful hypothetical construct and a hypothetical construct which will require revision.

In the winter of 1933, shortly after Hitler had, at the request of von Papen and von Hindenburg, become chancellor of Germany, French newspapers gave front-page coverage to an especially grotesque murder case in the south of France. In addition to drawing the usual journalistic publicity, the two murderesses, the Papin sisters, attracted the active interest of the political left. Sympathizers with the accused pair included Jean-Paul Sartre and Simone de Beauvoir, who were aroused by what appeared to be a quintessentially romantic, though repugnantly violent, rebellion of servants against masters.

Janet Flanner (who, by coincidence, wrote under the nom de plume *Genêt*) summarized the case for American readers.[14] She wrote that the Papin sisters, Christine (age 28) and Léa (age 21), were employed, respectively, as cook and housemaid in the home where M. Lancelin, an attorney in Le Mans, resided with his wife and daughter. Despite their difference in age, the two Papins were almost identical in appearance. On the evening of 2 February 1933, Christine brutally blinded her mistress, then cut her in pieces with a carving knife; Léa committed the same atrocities upon the Lancelin daughter. Having scattered their victims' body parts and put the furniture in frightening disarray, the pair withdrew to their attic room, taking time to cleanse themselves thoroughly before retiring. Upon their arrest, Christine said that they had repeatedly angered Mme Lancelin by using an electric iron that blew out the fuses and had just caused the electricity to go out once again when Mme Lancelin and her daughter had come in.[15]

During the ensuing trial, Flanner relates, Christine exhibited erratic behavior, sometimes ranting, sometimes speaking calmly but nonsensically, while Léa was not able to speak at all. Experts testified to the sisters' peculiar relationship, to their extraordinary closeness and incestuous homosexuality. It was established that they had suffered abuse as children and that during their six years of service, Mme Lancelin had remained curiously distant and strict, subjecting the maids' dusting and cleaning to a series of literal white-glove tests. The press reported the trial in gleefully appalled detail.

To hypothesize the original audience's responses to the incorporation of the Papins' story into *Les bonnes,* readers need to consider first whether or not the memory of these two notorious sisters remained in the minds of theatregoers. This was perhaps more likely with those who for political reasons had seen in them symbols for an entire underclass (much as some in the late 1980s saw in Hedda Nussbaum a symbol for all battered women) than for those who had merely read about them with horror in the newspapers. But let us assume that both groups did retain some knowledge of the case.[16]

The original audience, then, would have recognized that the play's maids do in fact resemble the Papin sisters. They would have noticed Claire's and Solange's incestuous passion for each other, their highly bizarre behavior, their ritualized plan for a vengeful murder, and their tendency to reflect or imitate each other. They would have seen, as well, in Solange's domination of Claire, a reminder of how Christine ruled Léa.

Yet they would have appreciated too the significant differences between the Papins and, as Genet renames them, the Lemerciers ("the merciful ones"). The Lemerciers' violent affections are not limited to each other, but extend to Mario, the seductive milkman to whom they obscurely and repeatedly refer; to Monsieur, their mistress's lover; and to Madame herself, whom they love as much as they loathe. Claire and Solange are closer in age and rank than their real-life counterparts, and just who is the stronger of the two shifts dramatically at the end of the play; certainly, Claire's final decision and suicide contrast very sharply with Léa's compliance and withdrawal into silence. Most obvious to this audience, however, would have been the fact that the murder itself, which the two sisters rehearse so fervently, is never committed. The killing of master by servant, which for the spectators would have formed the very basis of the Papin case, does not take place in *Les bonnes.*

Audiences would have observed too how the heavy politicization of the case of more than a decade before is thoroughly defused on stage. Unlike the actual Mme Lancelin, who during the six years in which the Papins worked for her never once spoke to them, communicating through formal notes instead, Madame in the play seems to the audience at the very worst patronizing, indifferent. Furthermore, Madame is not (as was Mme Lancelin) an epitome of middle-class respectability: she is, rather, a somewhat shadowy figure, perhaps a kept woman, possibly a demimondane. Her stinginess is offset by a capricious generosity, and her coldness is balanced by an intense warmth. And her servants, rather than being utter victims, seem at times in control not only of their psychotic game but, at least in the end, of some potent symbolic logic. The reflection in *Les bonnes* of the raging public controversy is eerily quiet and private.

In short, Genet's version of the Papin case forms something of a mirror image, an *inversion* of the original. As the audience of the first production would have noted, the maids' gruesome murder of their female superiors is refashioned by the play into a rehearsal for a murder that does not come off, into a ceremony that ultimately turns inward. Ultimately, it leads to the destruction and the irrevocable transformation of the maids themselves rather than of their mistress.

I submit that if the first audience of *Les bonnes* did not respond positively to the play, it was not because they could not respond to the Papin material, which was certainly not beyond their grasp. Rather, their negative responses to the play were, I would offer, more the result of their "reading" of the production even before they had set foot in the theatre. They would have constructed, based upon the circumstances surrounding the production, certain expectations about the play which the play itself ultimately disappointed. The play's director, its scene designer, the theatre in which it played, the other piece with which it appeared—all of these would have seemed, to the original spectators, to have promised a certain kind of experience in the theatre.

Much of the relevant production information is reproduced in the English translation. It indicates that *Les bonnes* was originally presented in April 1947 at the Théâtre de l'Athénée, and that it was directed by Louis Jouvet and designed by Christian Bérard (GP 33). What did this mean to the original audience—or, to pose this in a manner consistent with my thesis, what would the audience have done with this information? Theatregoers at the time would have thought of the Théâtre de l'Athénée as the home of the works of dramatist Jean Giraudoux, who had been produced at l'Athénée since 1934; in the season before *Les bonnes* opened, the playhouse had scored an enormous success with the premiere of Giraudoux's *La folle de Chaillot*. They would have known that this recent hit and almost every other play by Giraudoux (beginning with *Siegfried* in 1928) had been directed by Jouvet. Bérard had designed both *La folle de Chaillot* and Giraudoux's previous full-length play, *Sodome et Gomorrhe* (produced at the Théâtre Hébertot in 1943; this play was the only one by Giraudoux that was not directed by Jouvet).

If we add to all this one more piece of information indicated by numerous other sources—that *Les bonnes* was in fact paired on a double bill with a one-act play by Giraudoux, *L'Apollon de Marsac*[17]—it is difficult for us to avoid the conclusion that most of the members of the original audience went to the theatre anticipating, as was only natural, that they would be seeing a play that was in some way similar, or at least related to, the work of Giraudoux. Even with the help of Jouvet and Bérard and l'Athénée, however, spectators could not easily turn *Les bonnes* into something by the author of *Ondine* and *Intermezzo*.

How valid are the responses I have attributed to this audience I have hypothesized? I believe that if one can accept my two key assumptions—that these spectators were able to recall the Papin case and that they found the credits for the production significant—then the hypothetical-audience responses which I propose above are reasonable, even likely. Difficulty and doubt enter, I think, only when there is sound data to contradict the assumptions upon which the hypothetical audience has been constructed.

In hypothesizing about classical Greek or Elizabethan audiences, we may have to rely on very little real information and rather too many assumptions. With more recent spectators, though, we may be able to compare our assumptions with several facts that are available. In the next section, I will illustrate the construct of the actual audience by examining some hard evidence; and this, in turn, will test the validity of the assumptions which I have put forward.

An Actual Audience of "Les bonnes"

As I have defined it in chapter 4, the reader should think of the actual audience construct as a *re*construction. It is based upon specific, concrete, factual information which concerns a real audience's responses to an actual performance of a play. This information is drawn from various sources outside the playscript, sources such as reviews and notices, memoirs, diaries, and letters, and so on—indeed, any material that in some way describes the specific responses of real spectators may be included. There is, as I have noted, ample documentation available on many productions, but there seems to be remarkably little on what the audience actually did.

With regard to the spectators who attended the first production of *Les bonnes,* contemporary drama reviews published in newspapers and magazines and the memoir of one of the director's associates provide glimpses of them. Although the information these sources contain is meager, enough exists to allow a critique of the hypothetical constructs presented in the previous section. The *re*construction of the actual first audience permits us to fill in what has been until now only a vaguely sketched view of the role that these spectators played.

It is imperative to remember that relevant materials rarely come into being in order to record audience response. For example, drama notices carried in dailies and weeklies are for the most part written to negotiate in some way between what happens on stage and what happens in the house. Elizabeth Burns, in *Theatricality: A Study of Convention in the Theatre and Social Life,* sees the need for this kind of negotiation as intrinsic to theatre:

> There is a conflict that lies at the roots of the relationship between dramatist, actors and producers on the one side and on the other, the audience. The more closely they are drawn together the sharper the discrepancy between their interests, the more damaging the representation of the real in terms of the theatrical world.[18]

Nevertheless, Burns views the drama critic's position in this inevitable rift not as central but as opportunistic:

> In the larger society from which the audience is drawn, the theatre depends for its being on the preservation of a conception of drama that assigns it some position central to contemporary culture.
>   It is this centrality that the critic seeks to exploit. He is, in fact, not the spokesman of inarticulate spectators but a self-appointed mediator between the value system signified or articulated in a play and the values obtaining in contemporary society.[19]

In this sense, the critic, who usually appears to be paying attention to the dramatic and theatre texts, is also at the same time heeding the responses in the house; most critics, as adherents of object-oriented theories of art, seem to write only about what happens on stage. Thus, relatively few reviews *explicitly* reflect the critic's negotiatory role. The critic tends rather to obscure mediation and to act the very role of "spokesman of inarticulate spectators" which Burns discounts. Yet on occasion, when the responses of the spectators become an issue (which seems to have occurred during the first run of *Les bonnes*), reviewers feel obliged to record the audience's actions and reactions.

Similarly, the writer of a theatre memoir does not set out to document audience response. Yet, there are times when the audience cannot be ignored, or to be fair, cannot be rendered transparent or compliant. Thus, Léo Lapara, whose *Dix ans avec Jouvet* covers the period in which he worked with the famed director, describes in detail how audiences at the Théâtre de l'Athénée received what in the spring, summer, and fall of 1947 became a highly controversial double bill.

Both of these sources must be approached with caution. As Burns suggests, theatre critics, who are constantly positioning themselves at center stage, if only intellectually, are far from neutral. Likewise, a writer like Lapara, whose recollections are organized to memorialize the great reputation of Jouvet, is clearly prejudiced. Nonetheless, the information these sources contain remains highly useful.

In his comprehensive and illuminating review of virtually all the dramatic and literary notices in French of Genet's works, Richard Coe points out that only one critic of the original production of *Les bonnes*, Guy Joly (writing in *L'aurore*), connected the two domestics in the play with the Papin case.[20] "And admittedly," concludes Coe, "the subject of the Papin sisters was one of which many spectators whose memories went back as far as 1933, and who had a social conscience, would have preferred not to be reminded."[21]

Coe's deduction, which seems sound, invalidates my hypothesis built on the assumption that the first audiences recognized the play's references to the Papins. Still, his assertion that spectators "would have preferred not to be reminded" of the case only begins to explain audience response here. Having looked at the playscript with the Papin story in mind, I am puzzled by the audience's obliviousness to what appears to me and to other commentators, notably Sartre,[22] so obvious. What Coe is really saying is not that spectators did not remember the Papins but that they did not wish to be reminded. But how exactly does an audience actively evade recognizing so many pointed references?

To an extent, as Coe implies, we may admit that spectators saw themselves in a historical situation dominated by more recent events, "the aftermath of the War, the Resistance and the liberation. . . ."[23] Moreover, the politics of the time tended toward wider, more abstract issues; for example, just two weeks before the play opened, Charles DeGaulle launched (in a speech at Strasbourg) the Rassemblement du Peuple Français (RPF), which over the next few months grew into a major nationwide movement.[24]

Political interests, rather than gravitating toward an individual case, were directed toward far larger and certainly more generalized public issues.

At the same time, however, if a memory of the Papins did occur to audience members—and I cannot help thinking that on some level it must have—then they would have been likely to have disregarded it, to disassociate the comparisons to which these remembrances ought to have led, due partially to the way in which the play itself had been mounted. "Christian Bérard," Bettina Knapp recalls, "caricatured the 'style cocotte' of the early 1900's in his décor. . . ."[25] Because of this, at least one seasoned reviewer, Jean Tardieu (writing in *Action*), saw the setting not as Jouvet's or Bérard's but as the dramatist's: "Genêt [sic][26] has placed the action in 1900, which permits him to exaggerate his nightmare figures . . . ," he notes and then goes on to utilize what he assumes is the play's (rather than the production's) period to explain the dramatic text. Marcel Thiebault, reviewing the play in *Carrefour* and André Frank, summing up the season in *Le populaire de Paris* the following September (in a review unknown to Coe) also thought the time period denoted by the set significant enough to mention.[27]

If critics as experienced as these could "read" the play in this way, is it unlikely that spectators did the same? And even if Parisian theatregoers were experienced in recognizing ancient myths dramatized in modern or at least modernized contexts, as they had done with Jean Cocteau's *Orphée* and *La machine infernale,* Anouilh's *Euridice* and *Antigone,* and both Giraudoux's and Sartre's versions of the Electra myth, would they have been able to associate a play set at the turn of the century with a cause célèbre of the 1930s? Bérard's setting (as well as the *belle epoque* costumes) located the play thirty years before the murders at Le Mans, and Genet's own reworking of the details of the Papin case made the link between fiction and reality conveniently ambiguous and thereby tenuous.

Significantly, even those spectators for whom the Papin case had in 1933 taken on important political implications were, as a result of the war and the politics of engagement, no doubt undergoing some reevaluation of their earlier involvement. Simone de Beauvoir, writing in the 1950s about the case, describes the mood of those who had sympathized with the Papins. Her point of view here is consciously more mature and decidedly postwar:

> The papers told us that they were sexually involved with each other, and we mused on the caresses, and the hatred, that their lonely attic concealed. Yet when we read accounts of the preliminary hearing we were distinctly shaken: the elder sister was, beyond any doubt, suffering from acute paranoia, and the younger had become infected with the same disorder. We were therefore wrong in regarding their excesses as being due to the hand of rough justice, suddenly unleashed; they had, rather, struck more or less blindly, in a state of terror and confusion. We could not bring ourselves to believe this, and obstinately persisted in our admiration for them—though this did not stop our getting very cross when government psychiatrists pronounced them both of sound mind. . . . They condemned the elder to death; but two days after the verdict she had to be put in a straitjacket, and was interned in an asylum for the rest of her life. We conceded the evidence.[28]

There is in de Beauvoir's defense of the Papins something admirable: only a person sincerely intent on exposing the duplicity of society could assert, "The two sisters became both the instruments and the martyrs of justice in its grimmest guise."[29] At the same time, though, this reminiscence of her response to the crime conveys more than a touch of irony, which suggests that she had detected in her earlier perspective a certain idealism and naivete. For Sartre and for de Beauvoir, who more than two decades later could recall, "Most other crimes faded into insignificance when set beside the Le Mans murders,"[30] the Papins remained very real; however, as Coe suggests, perhaps for most of the spectators, the Papin sisters were not eminently memorable.

The unwillingness and inability, then, of the vast majority of theatregoers to recognize the Papins as Genet's title characters conveys a key to their responses. If Genet had hoped in writing *Les bonnes* that one way the house would be able to relate to it would be via the Papin story, then on this level the play was a failure. Of course, it is possible to read or watch *Les bonnes* without reference to the criminal sisters—it would appear that most audience members today, even in France, are unable to make the connection, and many of these still judge the play a success.[31] However, all the effort which, according to my previous hypothesis, the original spectators expended on relating elements in the script to something from real life, would have had to have been directed elsewhere.

Much of this effort was aimed against a play that many felt did not work. Indeed, that the play did not work was a notion which, according to at least two reviews and to Lapara, a succession of audiences seemed to share.

Lapara, who claims Jouvet was pressured by Cocteau and others into producing the play, adds that the director knew the double bill "would not have a long run." He says Jouvet began rehearsing *Dom Juan* two days after the first reading of *Les bonnes,* and, insists Lapara, "His presentiments proved exactly right."[32] Having defended the director, however, Lapara (who in fact played one of the minor roles in the Giraudoux play) chronicles in unusual detail how the house reacted over the course of the plays' six-month engagement:

The first few performances [the play opened on 19 April 1947] unrolled without incident. The audience contented itself with a show of hostility to Genêt's [sic] work—listened coldly and greeted the end with scarce and meager applause—and acclaiming more than reasonably the Giraudoux play. . . . Starting with the eighth performance, things deteriorated. And then, up until the last, rare were the evenings on which *Les Bonnes* was not the object, during the course of its performance, of jibes, jeers, snickers, or whistles. Finally, mixed in with the booing and whistling in response, there were a few bravos and some applause from Genêt's [sic] champions.

Each day carried with it a miniature version of the battle in *Hernani*. But the palm-branch of audience censure came back during the sixty-fourth performance, on Sunday, September 21, 1947, in the evening: the curtain fell on *Les Bonnes* in a glacial silence which no applause came to break.

It did not rise again.[33]

There remains a trace of defensiveness here: the audience's adoration for Giraudoux (Jouvet's favorite) is contrasted with its loathing for Genet (of whom Jouvet had been wary). Still, this is a strikingly clear description of the reception of *Les bonnes,* and it is substantiated by contemporary drama criticism.

Two drama critics refer directly to the house. J.-J. Rinieri, who according to Coe influenced Genet's later view of the play,[34-] confirms in his review (in *La NEF*) that the house was not pleased:

As soon as the curtain falls, whistling and booing begin. Why? It seems the audience would like to revenge itself for having been held captive for an hour by a play that has offended it deeply.[35]

As a critic for the magazine which had just the month before published Genet's first play, *Haute surveillance,* Rinieri actively mediated between house and stage. He defended *Les bonnes* on the grounds of artistic merit and of freedom of expression, decrying Jouvet's production of it even as he praised the dramatic text itself.[36] Similarly, though less aggressively, Thierry Maulnier, in *Revue de la pensée française,* attempted to reconcile the spectators' uproar with the play's virtues:

[T]he director of the Théâtre de l'Athénée has been able to give a chance to a new work, which by its originality of form, the affect and aggressiveness of its tone, the nearly unsustainable tension which it exacts upon the ill-prepared spectator, must disconcert and thus has disconcerted a large segment of the audience and provokes at the same time, every night, manifestations of hostility. . . .

. . . The play offends general audiences . . . by the way it goes about disturbing spectators' "uneasy consciences" about incidents concerning such humiliation [of servant by master] . . . .[37]

In arbitrating between play and public, Maulnier uses a very different strategy from Rinieri. He maintains that the audience's reactions are understandable and implies that the play, which he feels is of major importance, *should* upset spectators; he even tries to explain why audiences do not enjoy being upset by *Les bonnes.*

Lapara contends, supposedly in agreement with Jouvet, that *Les bonnes* was from the outset a shaky proposition and that audience responses proved this. Rinieri, on the other hand, justifies the play and condemns the booing philistines who do not understand it. Maulnier's implicit counter to the charge that the play does not work is that it does work—if anything, far too well—and that the audience members do not know quite what to do with their experiences. Lapara includes spectator response to bolster his charge that there was something wrong with Genet's play (rather than with Jouvet). While the majority of critics felt no difficulty in presenting their own views with the scornful public, both Rinieri and Maulnier, who belonged to the minority who liked the play, needed to address directly and thus document audiences' responses. Interestingly, the three corroborate each other.

Do these responses help to confirm or to deny my hypothesis that audiences came expecting to see a Giraudoux play and thus found *Les bonnes* utterly contrary to their expectations? Having seen my first hypothesis reversed by solid information, should I now anticipate the destruction of my second?

Lapara's report that the audience's dislike of the Genet play made them cheer "more than reasonably the Giraudoux play" supports my hypothesis. Furthermore, the two reviewers cited above call attention to the influence which the Giraudoux play had on the program as a whole. Maulnier observes that "an unpublished play by Giraudoux presented by Jouvet [would be] almost certainly an assured success."[38] Rinieri, who as we have already seen finds the audience at fault, chastises, "But one would not seriously think that it was *for* this entertainment [by Giraudoux] that the production [double bill] has been created."[39] Indeed, virtually all reviewers (with the exception of Henriette Brunot, who reviewed the plays separately in *Psyché: Revue international de psychoanalyse et des Sciences de l'homme*)[40] remarked upon the odd juxtaposition of *L'Apollon de Marsac* and *Les bonnes.* On the whole, critics preferred *L'Apollon,* even those who thought it of minor consequence.

According to Donald Inskip, *L'Apollon* had been written after Giraudoux had resigned his post in Marshall Pétain's ministry of information in 1940; the script was sent to Jouvet in Rio de Janeiro, where it was produced in 1942.[41] Thus, *L'Apollon de Marsac* belonged, at least in conceptualization, to the theatre of the Ger-

man occupation and the Nazi censor. Superficially, it depicted
fantasy, but if it had been presented five years before its actual
French debut, a Parisian audience might also have read it on a
symbolic level in which truth and patriotism subtly peeked
through the whimsy. Significantly, for all their approval of *L'Apollon,* the critics saw little of substance in it. Perhaps what made the
critics take it seriously was that it had been written by Giraudoux.

What happened, then, when the audience looked at the Genet
play? "Given the subject matter," writes Coe, ". . . most of the spectators seem to have forced themselves into a frame of mind, in
which they not only expected to see, but actually *saw,* a naturalistic
melodrama." It is true, as Coe points out, that a number of reviewers called *Les bonnes* naturalistic in style, but many others, as Coe
himself is aware, compared it to Cocteau and Mirbeau.[42] Unable
to ascertain the theatre conventions under which *Les bonnes* was
to be experienced, drama critics did their best to draw comparisons. If the Genet play did not compare well to other works, this
made it all the easier to condemn it as bad "Zola" (André Frank,
La populaire de Paris, a review unknown to Coe),[43] bad "Mirbeau"
(Roger Lannes, *Le Figaro littéraire*),[44] bad "Sartre" (Tardieu, *Action*),[45] or as Francis Ambriére in *L'opéra* (in a review unknown to
Coe) insisted, the work of "a poor man's Cocteau."[46]

Such associations are not as groundless as Coe would like us to
believe. And such attempts to identify *Les bonnes* for the public
were, after all, part of the critics' job. But the point here is that if
experienced reviewers did not know just where to place the work,
then audiences were even more at a loss to figure out where it
belonged. Unlike reviewers, however, spectators do not have to
arrive at any firm conclusions of what a play *is* like or is *supposed*
to be like. They can watch a performance and feel confused,
angry. This would, at least in part, account for the responses described by Lapara and others.

Moreover, although spectators did not know what *Les bonnes*
was, they were very sure what it was *not:* it was obviously *not* the
kind of play they expected to see on a bill directed by Jouvet at
l'Athénée—it was *not,* to put it mildly, a Giraudoux play. What
made it even worse for them was that they had come for Giraudoux and Jouvet, and Jouvet would eventually *do* Giraudoux
(the director performed the title role in *L'Apollon*), but first they
had to sit and wait, according to Ambiére's estimate, for forty
minutes while this work by Genet played out.[47] Thus, they whistled
and jeered.

To some extent, then, the audience's loud aversion to *Les bonnes* had not been provoked by the play itself (as Maulnier argues). Although Genet may have wanted to provoke and outrage the spectators, many were more put out at the notion that they had to sit through his play in order to get what they had paid for. In the light of information about the actual audience, my original hypothesis is upheld, even strengthened, but it also becomes more complex.

"By the time *Les bonnes* was revived," asserts Coe regarding the 1954 production, ". . . the intellectual and theatrical climate of Paris had changed radically, and the play was seen for what it is: not a demented socialistic tract, but a classic of 'pure theatre.'"[48] Even if we disregard Coe's assumption that reviewers in 1947 saw the play in social-realist terms and ignore the fact that the script for the 1954 production was different (longer, more developed) from the one used seven years earlier, we must question his underlying belief that audinces were better prepared in 1954 to accept the play "for what it is."

The play in 1947 was what it was, and it is difficult, having established the context of its original reception, to claim that the audiences were completely wrong. Maulnier's interpretation, that the play was deliberately written to outrage its spectators, may be reasonably extended to all of Genet's dramatic works. Many spectators found themselves watching *Les bonnes* and feeling a variety of intense emotions which they had never before felt in the presence of a play; how were they to know that this was precisely what Genet would, years later, say was central to his theatre? While Genet was learning how to become Genet-the-playwright and to write the kind of plays that he would later say he had already written, audiences were learning how to relate to this kind of theatre experience.

To some degree, too, the original audiences felt that what Julian Hilton describes as the "contracts" set up between the stage and the house[49] had been somehow violated, and justly so: Jouvet had put the Giraudoux play at the end of the bill precisely to keep them in the theatre. He was clever enough to anticipate that, if *Les bonnes* had followed *L'Apollon*, disenchanted spectators would simply get up and leave. Unfortunately, it seems that he had not (contrary to Lapara's apologia) foreseen that the audience would react so violently; as Jouvet waited in the wings for *L'Apollon* to begin, he himself must have witnessed again and again the audience's apathy and overt hostility. Rather than risk their departure, he had exacerbated their anger. Like the three characters in Sartre's claustrophobic hell in *Huis clos,* those in the house felt trapped, and they resented becoming a captive when what they most wanted was to feel captivated.

The role played by the original audiences of *Les bonnes,* then, was major, both in determining its immediate fate, its *succès de scandale* and notoriety, and in informing its dramatist about the nature of audiences, about which he, at least as a dramatist, had had no previous firsthand knowledge. Like the spectators, Genet himself learned what he did not like, and the example set by Jouvet and Bérard at l'Athénée undoubtedly stayed with him. Ironically, he came to agree with his first audiences that he had no business in the theatre of Giradoux. His two explanations about how the play should be performed, *Comment jouer <<les bonnes>>* (1963) and *Lettre à Pauvert sur les bonnes* (1954), which Coe believes is derived in part from Rinieri's 1947 review, almost completely contradict the theatre conventions found in the play-script. In this way, Genet invited directors to mount the play creatively, which in turn made it possible for audiences to revisit *Les bonnes* and to experience it in radically new and thus newly outrageous productions. A spectator who was shocked by *Les bonnes* in 1947 might thus see it again and again over the next forty years and be shocked afresh each time.

The quantity and quality of information about audience response has improved over the past twenty years. Anne-Marie Gourdon, in *Théâtre, Public, Perception,* includes in her studies of spectators at five different plays a fascinating discussion of the audience of Victor Garcia's French production of *Les bonnes.* The production was based on the Spanish production of which Genet himself firmly and publicly approved.[50] Gourdon also contributed a chapter on the perceptions of the spectator of *Les bonnes* to the book *Les voies de la création théâtrale-IV,* a large portion of which describes various aspects of the now classic Garcia production in French. This documentation is extremely helpful to scholars and readers alike; nonetheless, as Kirsten Nigro (citing Juan Villegas) reminds us, the process of studying a play's audience response is, in the end, perhaps best achieved through a series of studies. The more detailed the information, the more time one must spend examining it.

The time and space required for such a detailed study prevent me from using Gourdon's data here. The relatively small amount of information on the 1947 production of *Les bonnes* seems far more manageable. It also appears far more typical of what readers might encounter while searching for data about spectator response to plays of the last two centuries. Moreover, as illuminating as Gourdon's research is and as important as Garcia's presentation of the play has become, the problems of response presented by the original audience of *Les Bonnes* are, at least in dramatic terms, far more significant than those presented by audiences of later French productions. The spectators whom Gourdon studied had less difficulty with the dramatic text; like the reviewers of the 1954 production, whom Coe follows, audience members stopped criticizing the dramatic text and began noticing how it had been mounted. Or, if I may express their experience in a rather different way, one borrowed from Daphna Ben Chaim, the 1954 audience felt a sufficient amount of "distance" from the dramatic text to be able to appreciate it. Theatre, notes Ben Chaim, requires that spectators distinguish what they see before them from what they see in real life, that they "resist empathy, identification, loss of self";[51] at the same time, they must feel enough proximity in the theatre to experience some connection or engagement. In 1954 such a balance was perhaps struck, but to the audiences of 1947, *Les bonnes* felt too close or too far.

The responses of the 1947 audiences are so different from our own that they deserve reconstruction and analysis. They offer us new insight into the script itself and, perhaps even more important, into our own readings of it. By comprehending the meaningful role which the audience played, we come to know the playscript of *Les bonnes* as a play.

Speculating an Audience and Its Responses

The construct which I have named the "speculated audience" may spring from pure conjecture, but it incorporates crucial aspects of the rhetorical, hypothetical, and actual audience constructs. Thus, after coming up with a speculation about an audience that did not see the play or about a production that was never mounted, playreaders must involve themselves in the same processes they used in looking for the rhetorical "audience-in-the-script," in building the responses of the hypothetical house, and in locating (when possible) the real reactions of actual audiences.

In order to illustrate this construct, I have chosen to focus on one of the more celebrated and influential speculations about the play, one which concerns not only the production itself but ultimately extends to the audience as well. As I have mentioned earlier, Sartre in his essay on *Les bonnes* (originally included as an appendix to *Saint Genet* and added as a preface to the American translation of the play) claims that Genet intended that the play be performed by males.

> Genet says in *Our Lady of the Flowers:* "If I were to have a play put on in which women had roles, I would demand that these roles be performed by adolescent boys, and I would bring this to the attention of the spectators by means of a placard which would be nailed to the right or left of the sets during the entire performance."[52]

In a footnote here, Sartre explains that *Les bonnes* was originally played by women, but "this was a concession which Genet made to Louis Jouvet . . . ." Sartre then goes on to discuss the implications of this sort of casting. This he does by describing how *Les bonnes* would play:

> [W]hat appears behind the footlights is not so much a woman as Genet himself living out the impossibility of being a woman. We would see before us the effort, at times admirable and at times grotesque, of a youthful male body struggling under its own nature, and, lest the spectator be caught up in the game, he would be warned throughout [by the placard]—in defiance of all the laws of stage perspective—that the actors are trying to deceive him as to their sex. In short, the illusion is prevented from "taking" by a sustained contradiction between the effort of the actor . . . and the warning of the placard.[53]

Whether or not this idea really did first come from Genet, Sartre's premise and subsequent analysis of the production which he has in mind imply an interesting question: How *would* an audience have responded if *Les bonnes* had originally been done with actors rather than actresses?

With regard to the actual audience who saw the play as it was produced in 1947, we may dispose of this question relatively quickly. The spectators at l'Athénée would have thought an all-boy production thoroughly repellent, even less sufferable than the actual audiences found the play performed by women. Under these circumstances, the audiences drawn by Jouvet and Giraudoux would not have waited for *L'Apollon de Marsac*. *Les bonnes* played by boys would have quickly closed or perhaps would never even have opened, for we may doubt that Jouvet would have produced the play.

In this essay, Sartre occasionally refers vaguely to "the spectator," but he does not seem to mean the actual 1947 audience. Although the production he describes appears to be hypothetical, what "reading" he does provide of house "response" (or of the theatre text's "effects") is highly rhetorical. His unidentified "spectator" responds in exactly the way that the imagined production "intends" for "him" to respond. Sartre is perhaps more concerned here, as he is throughout *Saint Genet,* with reinventing both Genet and Genet's misunderstood works and with promoting his own corrective responses to Genet than with examining audience response to *Les bonnes.*

As we have seen, speculating about a general audience's responses in Sartre's theatre-of-the-mind proves to be a short exercise, for we know, as does Sartre, that the majority of audience members greeted the 1947 premiere, which was mounted far more conventionally than the proposed production, with overt hostility. Therefore, we may productively add to our speculations about a performance of an all-male *Les bonnes* yet another speculation about *who* might have been likely to remain in the house to see it. In a sense, we are thus incarnating Sartre's *rhetorical* reading: we let the playscript and its imagined production determine the spectators. If we can be more specific, the so-called audience-in-the-text may now emerge as a hypothetical construct.

If we allow our minds to imagine freely, we may think of asking Sartre and also Genet's other great champion, Cocteau, to organize a house for us. Indeed, with the auditorium filled with intellectuals, artists, and leftists, we may find an audience who would not only be sympathetic to the dramatic text but who would be able to tolerate the transvestitism (or as the French would say, *travesti*) of the performance text and the untraditional use of the placard.

Of course, this seriously diminishes the size of the audience and the length of the run. Since Jouvet has departed and *L'Apollon de Marsac* has been removed from the bill, we would probably do better to transfer the production from l'Athénée to a more intimate and less revered theatre, like the tiny Théâtre de Poche or the relatively tiny Théâtre de Noctambules (both of which, unlike l'Athénée, would in the years ahead play host to a good number of very unconventional theatre pieces). In fact, during the week in April 1947 in which *Les bonnes* opened, the Théâtre de Poche was dark, perhaps even available, and the Théâtre de Noctambules was playing *André Frére.*[54]

Let us suppose for the sake of argument that the small but select crowd gathered in the Théâtre de Poche does collectively react to the play as Sartre has predicted. This is hardly a surprise, for they have been brought into the auditorium precisely so that they will respond in this way. Yet what does such a response mean on a collective level beside the inevitably thunderous applause and shouts of "Bravo"?

To a degree, we can follow the path of response that Sartre has projected. The spectators are confronted by a spectacle of "derealization," and they watch and listen intently, interestedly. They experience alienation and a sense of frustration—indeed, everything that Sartre has said they would. Yet individually they experience far more; even as Sartre and the rest of the house think the very thoughts that appear in his essay, the father of existentialism turns to observe that various audience members are quietly arguing with each other, while others are staring at the stage, their faces disfigured with emotion.

Sartre notices that Jean Marais is smirking rather broadly; Cocteau, seated beside Marais, nudges him with his elbow and slightly, almost imperceptibly, shakes his head. A bespectacled man, whom Sartre recognizes as Lacan, leans forward and speaks into Simone de Beauvoir's ear. Nodding and grimacing, de Beauvoir turns to Sartre, and says, "Papins." Behind them, Lacan snorts, sighs, but continues to watch. Albert Camus, who has come in late and thrown himself into a seat at the back, squirms uncomfortably, crosses his legs, stifles a yawn, and just glares. Jean-Louis Barrault is considering doing Genet's *Haute surveillance*, and he seems impressed but uncomfortable. Madeleine Renaud has accompanied him; she watches with what appears to Sartre to be extreme amusement. Charles Dullin, down in the first row, sits transfixed and, at the same time, giddy, laughing hysterically at Madame's entrance. Just across the aisle from Sartre and seated next to a young man Sartre cannot place, Anais Nin grits her teeth and now says a little too loudly to her companion, "I'm glad Artaud isn't here to see this!"

Such speculation is perhaps amusing for its own sake. It is also a way of getting at some of the wider possibilities of response and, as a logical extension, of interpretation inherent in our speculations. Ultimately, the audience, as a group, must be viewed as a collection of individuals. When the parameters of spectator response are imposed by the playreader (as they are with Karen Laughlin's rhetorical audience), the playreader is merely projecting his or her own possibilities, that is, those possibilities conceivable to the reader. However, when those possibilities are prompted by the divergent or even contradictory points of view of a few key speculated spectators (some of whom even formed the actual audience), then readers' projections are guided, if only initially, by external and actual points of view.

Constructing the speculated audience is rather like creating a thought experiment. Readers may call in an invented house or play to an actual audience a made-up production in order to challenge a thesis or to support a point. The speculated audience is, of the four constructs proposed, the most sophisticated or at least the most difficult. It not only encompasses the other three constructs but demands that playreaders take a fully active role in conceptualizing the play in performance.

Conclusion

Reading *Les bonnes* with the audience in mind allows playreaders to view it in a variety of ways. Playreaders are, with the "assistance" (as Peter Brook would call it) of the imagined spectators, more acutely aware of responses that differ significantly from their own. Moreover, they may acquire, through continued audience-oriented study, a sense of the ongoing significance of the play.

For if, as Gross asserts, understanding playscripts is less a matter of responding to the meaning of the dramatic text and more a matter of responding to a text meaningfully, then playreaders may begin to see what we generally call *meaning* more as a continuum of how readers and spectators have responded meaningfully to a play since it was first read and seen. Playreaders may thus regard their own responses as part of an ongoing process; they may locate themselves among other "readers" and consider their own readings in the light of several years, or, as in the case of *Les bonnes,* of several decades of response.

My readings of *Les bonnes* have not been (nor were they intended to be) definitive and comprehensive. If a complete discussion of audience reception of the play had been my object here, I would have been obliged to look at far more than what I have, to go through or at least gesture toward the series of studies which Nigro tells us Villegas specifies. Instead, my goal throughout this section has been to exemplify the theatre-audience constructs which I have proposed and to present sample readings of an important playscript.

If the rhetorical construct permits playreaders an opportunity to fill their mental playhouses with an audience that always agrees with their own readings, the hypothetical construct forces readers to step out of the theatre seats and to take on a position that is not necessarily allied with either the stage or the house. The actual audience allows readers to reestablish a house that actually came, saw, and responded to the play in question, if such a house ever existed. The speculated house lets playreaders juggle time and space in an attempt to make sense of possible responses.

The purpose of these constructs is to guide playreaders not toward the correct reading but toward a corrective kind of reading. The playreaders' audiences are proposed not to restrict readers but to extend their abilities to read playscripts, to—in the academese of the late 1980s—empower them.

Notes

Chapter 1. Introduction

1. Jorge Luis Borges, *Labyrinths: Selected Short Stories and Other Writings,* ed. Donald A. Yates and James E. Irby (New York: New Directions, 1964), 248.

2. Quoted by Andrew Gurr in *Playgoing in Shakespeare's London* (Cambridge: Cambridge University Press, 1987), 241. Gurr quotes Baker (in *Theatrum Redivivum*), citing Martin Butler's *Theatre and Crisis 1632–1642* (Cambridge: Cambridge University Press, 1984).

3. Ibid., 192. Again, Gurr is drawing from Butler. Lord Falkland's letter (to Thomas Carew) was written in the 1630s.

4. See Gary Vena, *How to Read and Write About Drama,* 2d ed. (New York: Arco-Simon & Schuster, 1984), for the earliest use of this term.

5. Roger Gross, *Understanding Playscripts: Theory and Method* (Bowling Green, Ohio: Bowling Green University Press, 1974), 4–5; Kirsten Nigro, "On Reading and Responding to (Latin American) Playtexts," *Gestos* 2 (November 1987), 101–2.

6. Thelma Altschuler and Richard Paul Janow, *Responses to Drama: An Introduction to Plays and Movies* (Boston: Houghton Mifflin, 1967), 81.

7. Thomas R. Whitaker in *Fields of Play in Modern Drama* (Princeton: Princeton University Press, 1977), 6–7, prefaces his playful performances of close readings of playscripts with a similar comparison:

> Scripts, like musical scores, are normative invitations. And though a major script leaves open a wide range of directorial choices and audience responses, it implies with some precision not only the "objectives" and "subtexts" of the *dramatis personae* but also the lines of action and sequences of perception to be shared by the implied participants.

Whitaker's conclusion here, that the playscript to some degree determines the audience's responses, is an extremely interesting one; however, by failing to specify just how powerful this "precision" actually is, the reader is left—perhaps erroneously—with the notion that the audience is by and large passive.

Bernard Beckerman, in *Theatrical Presentation: Performer, Audience and Act,* ed. Gloria Brim Beckerman and William Coco (New York: Routledge, 1990), 74, offers a similar (though nonmusical) analysis of performance and response:

> Not every show is designed to arouse both simple and complex responses, nor is it capable of so doing. Those shows that can evoke complex responses can also incorporate simple responses within them. The opposite is not the case, however. Shows primarily designed . . . to produce simple responses, exclude the possibility of complex response.

This idea, that there is something intrinsic in what Beckerman calls "the show" which determines the house response, leads to a discussion in which, even though they are described as doing something, the spectators remain the object of the play, allegedly active and at the same time rather passive (Beckerman, *Theatrical Presentation,* 80–81). Thus, his example of Ibsen's *A Doll's House,* places the audience in an odd position: "For an audience rooted in nineteenth-century beliefs in the supremacy of the family, Nora's challenge to Torvald is a challenge to its own values" (Beckerman, *Theatrical Presentation,* 85).

8. Stephen Greenblatt, *Shakespearean Negotiations: The Circulation of Social Energy in Renaissance England* (Berkeley: University of California Press, 1988), 6.

9. Harry Berger, Jr., *Imaginary Audition: Shakespeare on Stage and Page* (Berkeley: University of California Press, 1989), xii.

10. Michael Issacharoff and Robin F. Jones, eds., *Performing Texts* (Philadelphia: University of Pennsylvania Press, 1988), 1.

11. Austin E. Quigley, *The Modern Stage and Other Worlds* (New York: Methuen, 1985), 4–5.

12. Like Aristotle's Greek, our language has no single term that describes those who see and hear the play. As Gurr notes, "English lacks an adequate word for the feast of the senses which playgoing ought to provide. . . . There is no English term which acknowledges the full experience of both hearing and seeing the complete 'action' of a play" (Gurr, *Playgoing,* 85). Peter Brook, in *The Empty Space* (New York: Atheneum, 1968), 139, offers a French term, *l'assistance,* to describe those in the house. For the most part in this study I use *audience* and *spectators* interchangeably.

Although current usage permits *audience,* as a collective noun, to be used as either a singular or a plural, for the sake of consistency I have tried to defer throughout this study to common American usage which, unlike British, prefers the singular. Nonetheless, I do not mean to imply by this that an audience is a singular mass which acts in complete unison; in most situations audiences ought to be thought of as many diverse people with differing views.

13. Marvin Carlson, *A Theatre Semiotics: Signs of Life* (Bloomington: University of Indiana Press, 1990), 10–11.

14. Tom Stoppard, *Rosencrantz and Guildenstern Are Dead* (New York: Grove, 1967), 64.

15. Alfred Harbage, *Shakespeare's Audience* (New York: Columbia University Press, 1941), 6.

16. Susan Bennett, "The Role of the Theatre Audience: A Theory of Production and Reception" (Diss., McMaster University, 1988), 5.

17. Herbert Blau, *The Audience* (Baltimore: Johns Hopkins University Press, 1990), 6.

18. Susan Bennett maintains that experimental theatre alone allows spectators the opportunity to function actively and that conventional theatre demands that audience members enter into a "social contract" in which they accept a "passive role" (see Bennett, "Theatre Audience," 347). I disagree with this premise, for even when productions demand that the audience play a reactive role, there are not only times during the performance when the dramatic and theatre texts allow and encourage more active participation but also times when the audience members themselves decide to break the contract. Such times are not merely occasional: they are always at the very least imminent and thus comprise, if only in their potentiality, a major part of the audience's experience.

19. I offer a discussion of what *reader-response* means, or at least of what has been meant by the term and what I mean by it, at the beginning of chapter 3.

20. Nigro, "On Reading," 101.

21. Marvin Carlson, *Theories of the Theatre: A Historical and Critical Survey, from the Greeks to the Present* (Ithaca: Cornell University Press, 1984), 166.

22. Ibid., 182.

23. Anne Ubersfeld, *Lire le théâtre* (Paris: Editions Sociales, 1977), and *L'ecole du spectateur: Lire le théâtre II* (Paris: Editions Sociales, 1982).

23. I follow Keir Elam in differentiating the dramatic text and the theatre (or performance) text. As Elam puts it, "'Theatre' is taken to refer here to the complex of phenomena associated with the performer-audience transaction: that is, with the production and communication of meaning in the performance. . . . By 'drama', on the other hand, is meant that mode of fiction designed for stage representation and constructed according to particular ('dramatic') conventions." The playscript, which is written or at least "composed *for* the theatre," is a dramatic text. See Keir Elam, *The Semiotics of Theatre and Drama* (London: Methuen, 1980), 2–3.

24. This sense of "play" is very much lacking in some of the more brilliant yet rigidly object-oriented theorists. For example, Michael Kirby, in *A Formalist Theatre* (Philadelphia: University of Pennsylvania Press, 1987), xi, insists that crucial to any definition of theatre is the "intent to make something that will affect an audience." His formalist and structuralist approach is extremely useful, especially when the main concerns are not only "with content-laden 'drama' but with performances" (Kirby, x). But at the same time, those given an active role to play are seemingly not those seated in the audience.

Chapter 2. The Literature of Playreading

1. J. L. Styan, *The Elements of Drama* (Cambridge: Cambridge University Press, 1960), 1.

2. Ibid., 3.

3. Anthony Leonard Manna, "An Exploration of a Stage-Centered Method of Teaching Dramatic Literature with a Group of Prospective Secondary School Teachers of English" (Diss., University of Iowa, 1976), 2.

4. The second (1947) edition of Cleanth Brooks's and Robert B. Heilman's *Understanding Drama* (New York: Holt, 1945) changed slightly. This later version was one of two works dealing with literary theory that was still widely read in Canadian colleges when, in 1973, Michael Holden wrote his dissertation on textbooks with which students training to become secondary teachers were familiar. See Michael Dennis Holden, "Literary Theory and the Education of English Teachers: An Analysis of Theories of Literature Presented in Selected Texts on Literature and Its Teaching" (Diss., University of Toronto, 1973).

5. Frank Lentricchia, *After the New Criticism* (Chicago: University of Chicago Press, 1980), xii–xiii.

6. Terry Eagleton, *Literary Theory: An Introduction* (Minneapolis: University of Minnesota Press, 1983), 47.

7. Roger Gross, *Understanding Playscripts: Theory and Method* (Bowling Green, Ohio: Bowling Green University Press, 1974), 8.

8. Ibid., 7.

9. Ibid., 9.

10. Richard Hornby, *Script into Performance: A Structuralist Approach* (New York: Paragon, 1977), 19–20.

11. Marvin Carlson, *Theories of the Theatre: A Historical and Critical Survey, from the Greeks to the Present* (Ithaca: Cornell University Press, 1984), 403.

12. Brooks and Heilman, *Understanding Drama*, ix.

13. Ibid., x.

14. These anthologies are mentioned by Brooks and Heilman throughout their discussions of the fifteen plays which they analyze but do not include (in Appendix A, 453–79). I cite them only from the editors' citations.

15. Brooks and Heilman, *Understanding Drama*, x.

16. Ibid., 479–84.

17. Ibid., 9.

18. Ibid., 11.

19. Ibid., 25–26.

20. Ibid., 33.

21. Gerald F. Else, *Aristotle's Poetics: The Argument* (Cambridge: Harvard University Press, 1957), 278.

22. Aristotle, *The Poetics*, Loeb Classical Library ed., trans. Hamilton Fyfe (Cambridge: Harvard University Press, 1927), 29.

23. Brooks and Heilman, *Understanding Drama*, 485–86.

24. Ibid., 468.

25. Ibid., 485–86.

26. Jean Cocteau, "Preface to *Les mariés de la Tour Eiffel*," in *Playwrights on Playwriting*, ed. Toby Cole (New York: Hill & Wang, 1961), 242.

27. Mortimer J. Adler and Charles Van Doren, *How to Read a Book*, rev. ed. (New York: Simon & Schuster, 1972), 223.

28. Kenneth Thorpe Rowe, *A Theater in Your Head* (New York: Funk & Wagnalls, 1960), 5.

29. Ibid., 5.

30. Ibid., 9.

31. Ibid., 10.

32. Rowe explains his inclusion of Ward's *Our Lan'* as follows: "it is a truly fine play that has been produced and reviewed with high praise, but with a comparatively short run and not hitherto published it offers experience of a new play for most readers" (ibid., 256). Rowe worked with Ward during the revision process and gives a brief summation of the play's history. He also encourages readers to recite the play aloud "for the quality and effect of the speech to become established to the ear" (ibid., 260).

33. Ibid., 429–30.

34. Ibid., 430.

35. Ibid., 9.

36. Ibid., 112.

37. Ibid., 141.

38. Ibid., 112.

39. Ibid., 4.

40. Bernard Grebanier, *Playwriting: How To Write for the Theater* (New York: Barnes & Noble, 1961), 5.

41. Ibid., 51.

42. Ibid., vii.

43. Gary Vena, *How to Read and Write About Drama*, 2d ed. (New York: Arco-Simon & Schuster, 1984), 9.

44. Ibid., 86–87.

45. Ibid., 108–11.

46. Christopher Russell Reaske, *How to Analyze Drama* (New York: Monarch, 1966), 81–85.

47. Ibid., 92–93.

48. G. B. Tennyson, *An Introduction to Drama* (New York: Holt, 1967), 99.

49. Robert F. Whitman, *The Play-Reader's Handbook* (New York: Bobbs-Merrill, 1966), 7–8.

50. Thelma Altschuler and Richard Paul Janow, *Responses To Drama: An Introduction to Plays and Movies* (Boston: Houghton Mifflin, 1967), 81.

51. Ronald Hayman, *How to Read a Play* (New York: Grove, 1977), 9.

52. Ibid., 11.

53. Ibid., 17–22.

54. Ibid., 30–38.

55. Ibid., 56–60.

56. Ibid., 93.

57. J. L. Styan, *The Dramatic Experience: A Guide to the Reading of Plays* (Cambridge: Cambridge University Press, 1965), ix.

58. Ibid., ix.

59. Ibid., 3.

60. Ibid., 110.

61. Ibid., 3.

62. Ibid., 8.

63. Ibid., 1.

64. Ibid., 2.

65. Ibid., 8.

66. Ibid., 15.

67. Hayman, *How to Read a Play,* 11.

68. Styan does include at the end of *The Dramatic Experience,* under "Basic Reading Lists," several excellent bibliographies. However, none of the books included are mentioned in the text itself.

69. Gross, *Understanding Playscripts,* iv.

70. Ibid., vii.

71. Ibid., x.

72. Ibid., xii.

73. Ibid., 22.

74. Ibid.

75. Ibid., 23.

76. Ibid., 35.

77. Ibid., 40–44.

78. Ibid., 44–48.

79. Ibid., x.

80. Ibid., 51–52.

81. Ibid., 79.

82. Ibid., 138–39.

83. Ibid., 134.

84. Ibid., 22.

85. Ibid., 134.

86. Ibid., ix.

87. Ibid., x.

88. See Robert Scholes, *Structuralism in Literature* (New Haven: Yale University Press, 1974).

89. Reader-response criticism was not as easy to come by when Gross wrote

Understanding Playscripts in 1974. In addition to I. A. Richards, whom Gross quotes, and Louise Rosenblatt, whom few outside education knew, only a few works which we would today associate with mainstream reader-response criticism were readily available in the United States. Some of the more familiar include Fish's *Surpris'd by Sin* (1967), *Self-Consuming Artifacts* (1972), and some of the articles that would later go into *Is There a Text in This Class?* (1980); Holland's *The Dynamics of Literary Response* (1968) and *Poems in Persons* (1973); Ingarden's *The Literary Work of Art* (1973); and articles by Iser, Poulet, and Riffaterre.

This list is drawn from Elizabeth Freund's 1987 study of reader-response criticism; see *The Return of the Reader: Reader-Response Criticism* (New York: Methuen, 1987), 165–73. Significantly, in 1974 the term *reader-response* had yet to be attached to those whom I name above.

90. My telephone conversation with Dr. Gross took place on the afternoon of 2 August 1988.

91. Gross, *Understanding Playscripts*, 149.

92. Ibid., 7.

93. Ibid., 135.

94. Ibid., 94.

95. Ibid., 83.

96. Jeremy Campbell, *Grammatical Man: Information, Entropy, Language, and Life* (New York: Simon & Schuster, 1982), 179.

97. Gross, *Understanding Playscripts*, 58–59.

98. Ibid., 120.

99. Ibid., 7.

100. Ibid., 89.

101. Ibid., 122.

102. Ibid., 3.

103. Ibid., 81–82.

104. Ibid., 198.

105. Ibid., 210–11.

106. Carlson, *Theories of the Theatre*, 490.

107. Hornby, *Script into Performance*, 5.

108. Ibid., 4.

109. Ibid., 11.

110. Elam, *The Semiotics of Theatre and Drama*, 217.

111. Hornby, *Script into Performance*, 66.

112. Ibid., 69.

113. Ibid., 9.

114. Ibid., 5.

115. Ibid., 8.

116. Robert Gardner, "The Dramatic Script and Procedural Knowledge: A Key to the Understanding of Dramatic Structure and a Foundation for the Development of Effective Curriculum Design in Dramatic Instruction at the Tertiary Level" (Diss., University of Toronto, 1983), iv.

117. Ibid., 408.

118. Gross, *Understanding Playscripts*, 39.

119. Ibid., 407.

120. David Grote, *Script Analysis: Reading and Understanding the Playscript for Production* (Belmont, Calif.: Wadsworth, 1985), v.

121. Ibid., 22.

122. Ibid., 217.

123. Ibid., 145.
124. Ibid.
125. Ibid.
126. Ibid., 223.
127. Ibid., 169.
128. David Scanlan, *Reading Drama* (Mountain View, Calif.: Mayfield, 1988), 1.
129. Ibid., iii.
130. Ibid., 22.
131. Ibid., 170.
132. Ibid., 17.
133. Ibid., 18.
134. Ibid., 18.
135. As this book was going to press, a new volume of essays on reading drama appeared; see *Reading Plays: Interpretation and Reception,* ed. Hannah Scolnicov and Peter Holland (New York: Cambridge University Press, 1991).

Chapter 3. Playreading and the Reader-Response Critics

1. Kirsten Nigro, "On Reading and Responding to (Latin American) Playtexts," *Gestos* 2 (November 1987), 101.
2. Robert C. Holub, *Reception Theory: A Critical Introduction* (New York: Methuen, 1984), xii.
3. Jane P. Tompkins, "An Introduction to Reader-Response Criticism," in Jane P. Tompkins, ed., *Reader-Response Criticism: From Formalism to Post-Structuralism* (Baltimore: Johns Hopkins University Press, 1980), ix.
4. Susan Suleiman, "Introduction: Varieties of Audience-Oriented Criticism," in Susan Suleiman and Inge Crossman, eds., *The Reader in the Text: Essays on Audience and Interpretation* (Princeton: Princeton University Press, 1980), 6.
5. Stephen J. Mailloux, *Interpretive Conventions: The Reader in the Study of American Fiction* (Ithaca: Cornell University Press, 1982), 20.
6. Elizabeth Freund, *The Return of the Reader: Reader-Response Criticism* (New York: Methuen, 1987), 10.
7. Peter J. Rabinowitz, "'What's Hecuba to Us?' The Audience's Experience of Literary Borrowing," in Susan Suleiman and Inge Crossman, eds., *The Reader in the Text: Essays on Audience and Interpretation* (Princeton: Princeton University Press, 1980), 243.
8. Rabinowitz, "'What's Hecuba to Us?'" 243–44.
9. See Peter J. Rabinowitz, *Before Reading: Narrative Conventions and the Politics of Interpretation* (Ithaca: Cornell University Press, 1987).
Rabinowitz's other major (though nonliterary) interest is music. In "Circumstantial Evidence: Musical Analysis and Theories of Reading," published five years after his essay appeared in the Suleiman and Crossman anthology, Rabinowitz amends some of his earlier ideas, adding to the concept of authorial and narrative audiences that of authorial and narrative "circumstances." He also indicates that knowledge about Aeschylus' *Libation Bearers* makes up part of the "authorial circumstances" for the authorial (reader) audience of Euripides' *Electra,* although he fails to relate this to the narrative (spectator) audience; see "Circumstantial Evidence: Musical Analysis and Theories of Reading," *Mosaic: A Journal for the Interdisciplinary Study of Literature* 18 (Fall 1985), 161. (Just this

narrative audience, Rabinowitz has previously told us, "can have no previous knowledge of the Electra story"; see "'What's Hecuba to Us?'" 258n.

In an earlier article, "Truth in Fiction: A Reexamination of Audiences," *Critical Inquiry* 4 (Autumn 1977): 121–41, Rabinowitz mentions a fourth audience, the "ideal," which "believes the narrator, accepts his judgments, sympathizes with his plight, laughs at his jokes even when they are bad" ("Truth in Fiction," 134). Although he indicates early in the essay that his "model is centered less on the novel's text than on the novel's reader" ("Truth in Fiction," 123), his remarks about audience ambiguities suggest that he sees these audiences not so much as the constructs of readers as the projections of the novels themselves. When Rabinowitz, toward the close, asserts that his "method can be adapted to drama as well" ("Truth in Fiction," 140), he never mentions whether it might be useful for the spectator or the reader; however, his next paragraph, in which he discusses performed program music ("Truth in Fiction," 140–41), and an earlier comparison between the viewer of *Othello* and the reader of a Sherlock Holmes story ("Truth in Fiction," 125) imply quite heavily that he is not at all concerned with the playreader here.

10. Rabinowitz, "'What's Hecuba to Us?'" 244.

11. Stanton Garner, although he never mentions Rabinowitz, contradicts the entire notion of "theatre narration" in novelistic terms in his introduction to *The Absent Voice:* "On the more fundamental levels of perception and cognition, and in terms of narrational function, the author's presence is *not* felt in the theater as it is felt in so many ways within the printed text"; see *The Absent Voice: Narrative Comprehension in the Theater* (Urbana: University of Illinois Press, 1989), xiv.

While this implies that playreaders at least have the assistance of a mediating voice, Garner later suggests that readers of playscripts encounter the dramatic text in a very different form than spectators who encounter the play on stage. The playscript, Garner asserts in reference to opening set descriptions and stage directions, "subtly misrepresents the theatrical moment as the audience initially experiences it . . . ." (4) According to Garner's thinking on this, the playreader who wishes to understand the play as the audience would must be able to translate the set description not into a complete and perfectly realized tableau but into a picture that evolves as the action proceeds. For Garner, as for so many others, reading plays cannot and must not be likened to reading novels.

12. Terry Eagleton, *Literary Theory: An Introduction* (Minneapolis: University of Minnesota Press, 1983), 51.

13. Louise M. Rosenblatt, *The Reader, the Text, the Poem: The Transactional Theory of the Literary Work* (Carbondale: Southern Illinois University Press, 1978).

14. Stanley E. Fish, *Is There a Text in This Class? The Authority of Interpretive Communities* (Cambridge: Harvard University Press, 1980).

15. Wolfgang Iser, *The Act of Reading: A Theory of Aesthetic Response* (Baltimore: Johns Hopkins University Press, 1978).

16. Rabinowitz's problem here is largely due to his dependence on S. H. Butcher's translation of Aristotle's *Poetics;* the considerable difficulties arising from critics' use of this translation are discussed in the final section of this chapter.

17. Rabinowitz, "'What's Hecuba to Us?'" 258n.

18. Ibid., 245.

19. Wolfgang Iser, "The Art of Failure: The Stifled Laugh in Beckett's Theater," *Bucknell Review* 26 (1981), 139–189.

20. David Bleich, *Subjective Criticism* (Baltimore: Johns Hopkins University Press, 1978), 126–28.

21. See Susan Elliot, "Fantasy Behind Play: A Study of Emotional Responses to Harold Pinter's *The Birthday Party, The Caretaker,* and *The Homecoming"* (Diss. University of Indiana, 1973).

Bleich was Elliot's dissertation advisor, and both his own work (including his then-unpublished *Subjective Criticism,* which she read in manuscript) and Norman Holland's served as major influences on her readings. Elliot (114) quotes from Holland's *Psychoanalysis and Shakespeare* (New York: McGraw-Hill, 1964), 313: "a play does not simply depict the stimuli and responses for some hypothetical and imaginary people—it *is* the stimulus to the responses of some very real people, the audience, among them the critic himself." For both Elliot and Holland, however, the responses of these "very real people" are identified with the responses of the reader. Thus, Elliot's commentary on Pinter's plays, in spite of her frequent references to individual theatre and literary critics, emphasizes (with true Bleichian subjectivity) Elliot's very private and very personal thoughts as reader and spectator. She does not look at the responses of actual audiences.

22. Rosenblatt, *The Reader,* 13.

23. Norman Holland, *The Dynamics of Literary Response* (New York: Norton, 1968), 174.

24. Ibid., 176.

25. Ibid., 179.

26. Ironically, Holland's first book dealt with eleven plays of the Restoration, and his second was an introduction to Shakespeare's works. Thus, his original "predominating genre" was drama. Significantly, his approach in both shows the influence of the criticism he would later repudiate. In *The First Modern Comedies: The Significance of Etheridge, Wycherley and Congreve* (Cambridge: Harvard University Press, 1959), he argues that the Restoration comedy is readily accessible to the sensibilities of modern readers, even those who know nothing of the period. In *The Shakespearean Imagination* (Bloomington: University of Indiana Press, 1964), 33, he equates the readings of the historical critic with those of the New Critic: "Both schools of thought embody that most distinctive trait of all twentieth-century thinking (not just Shakespeare criticism): concern for language." Neither book anticipates the author of *The Dynamics of Literary Response* (1968).

Holland's third book, as mentioned in note 21, helped shape Elliot's dissertation on Pinter. The book was written when, as Holland has more recently said of himself (in his "Afterword," in Sidney Homan, ed., *Shakespeare and the Triple Play: From Study to Stage to Classroom* [Lewisburg, Pa.: Bucknell University Press, 1988], 226), "he was behaving more like a Shakespearean and less like a reader-response critic." *Psychoanalysis and Shakespeare* seems today a transitional work. Nonetheless, throughout Holland's study, which attempts to put together and then follow a Freudian theory of literary response to Shakespeare's works, he repeatedly emphasizes those activities *shared* by spectators and reader, thus avoiding an examination of responses that differentiate the former from the latter.

27. Jane Tompkins, "The Reader in History: The Changing Shape of Literary Response," in Jane P. Tompkins, ed., *Reader-Response Criticism: From Formalism to Post-Structuralism* (Baltimore: Johns Hopkins University Press, 1980), 201.

Mary Louise Pratt, in "Interpretive Strategies/Strategic Interpretations: On Anglo-American Reader-Response Criticism," *Boundary 2* (Fall-Winter 1981–82),

201–31 (which is discussed in the next paragraph of text) agrees with Tompkins on the nature of the reader-response debt to formalism. I still have serious reservations about Tompkins's assertions on the primacy of interpretation. As I argue in chapter 4, many critics, notably structuralists and semiologists, seem more interested in exploring how a novel or playscript works rather than in what it means. Thus, they defer interpretation or avoid it entirely.

Interestingly, Norman Rabkin, in introducing the collected papers of the 1969 English Institute from which Stephen Booth's essay (discussed later in this chapter) is drawn, lauded the influence of innovative critics, such as Stanley Fish and Barbara H. Smith, with the pronouncement, "[T]he writers are freed from the increasingly deadening obligation to reduce works to meanings . . . ."; see Rabkin's "Foreword" in Norman Rabkin, ed., *Reinterpretations of Elizabethan Drama: Selected Papers from the English Institute* (New York: Columbia University Press, 1969), vii.

Perhaps the real legacy of the New Criticism to later critics (virtually all of whom were trained in New Critical method) is not so much Tompkins's notion that "interpretation is the only activity that will be recognized as doing what criticism is supposed to do" (Tompkins, "Reader in History," 225), but the *manner* of reading that New Critics taught in schools and universities, namely close reading.

28. Pratt, "Interpretive Strategies," 201.

29. Una Chaudhuri, "The Spectator in Drama/Drama in the Spectator," *Modern Drama* 27 (September 1984), 282.

30. Ibid.

31. Stephen Booth, "On the Value of *Hamlet*," in Norman Rabkin, ed., *Reinterpretations of Elizabethan Drama: Selected Papers from the English Institute* (New York: Columbia University Press, 1969), 136–76.

32. Mardi Valgamae, "Drama as an Art Form: Four Critical Approaches," *Journal of Baltic Studies* 12 (Winter 1981), 333–39.

33. Karen Laughlin, "Beckett's Three Dimensions: Narration, Dialogue, and the Role of the Reader in *Play*," *Modern Drama* 28 (1985), 329–40, and "'Looking for sense . . .': The Spectator's Reponse to Beckett's *Come and Go*," *Modern Drama* 30 (1987), 137–46.

34. Shoshona Weitz, "Reading for the Stage: The Role of the Reader-Director," *ASSAPH: Studies in the Arts (Sec. C)* 2 (1985), 122–41.

35. Tim Fitzpatrick, "Playscript Analysis, Performance Analysis—Towards a Theoretical Model," *Gestos* 1 (Nov. 1986), 13–28.

36. Nigro, "On Reading," 101.

37. Ibid., 110n.

38. Suleiman, "Introduction," 12.

39. Anne Ubersfeld, *Lire le théâtre* (Paris: Editions Sociales, 1977), and *L'école du spectateur: Lire le théâtre 2* (Paris: Editions Sociales, 1982).

40. Martin Esslin, *The Field of Drama: How the Signs of Drama Create Meaning on Stage and Screen* (New York: Methuen, 1987), 128.

41. Nigro, "On Reading," 101.

42. Norman Rabkin, "Foreword," ix.

43. Ibid., viii.

44. Ibid., vii–viii.

45. Mailloux, *Interpretive Conventions*, 70.

46. Booth, "On the Value of *Hamlet*," 142.

47. Mailloux, "Interpretive Conventions," 70.

48. Booth, "On the Value of Hamlet," 139.

49. Ibid., 140.

50. Ibid., 141.

51. William Gruber, *Comic Theaters: Studies in Performance and Audience Response* (Athens: Univerity of Georgia Press, 1986).

52. Sidney Homan, *The Audience as Actor and Character: The Modern Theatre of Beckett, Brecht, Genet, Ionesco, Pinter, Stoppard, and Williams* (Lewisburg, Pa.: Bucknell University Press, 1989), ii.

53. Laughlin, "Beckett's Three Dimensions," 338.

54. Laughlin, "Looking for Sense," 137.

55. Ibid., 138.

56. Ibid., 139–40.

57. Ibid., 142.

58. Ibid., 143.

59. Ibid., 144.

60. Ibid.

61. Ibid., 146n.

62. Nigro, "On Reading," 103.

63. Ibid.

64. Ibid., 104.

65. Ibid.

66. Ibid., 110n.

67. Ibid., 111n.

68. Ibid., 105–8.

69. Ibid., 108–9.

70. Ibid., 109.

71. Ibid.

72. Valgamae, "Drama as an Art Form," 336.

73. Ibid., 333.

74. Ibid., 334.

75. Ibid., 335–36.

76. I do not agree with Valgamae's "reading" of the fifth-century audience of *Lysistrata,* nor do I concur with his conclusion that a Soviet audience would have seen Saluri's *Who Am I?* as patriotic and thus pro-Soviet, while a Western audience might have viewed it as anti-Soviet; the audience behind the iron curtain would perhaps have best appreciated the play's subversive messages. The play's composition *in* Estonian would have been viewed by many as subversive to Soviet rule. However, as I have mentioned earlier, what I find interesting here are Valgamae's theoretical, not his interpretive, points.

77. Valgamae, "Drama as an Art Form," 338.

78. Bleich, *Subjective Criticism,* 98–99.

79. Rosenblatt, *The Reader,* 55.

80. Holland, *Dynamics of Literary Response,* 274, 298, 333.

81. Norman Holland, *5 Readers Reading* (New Haven: Yale University Press, 1975), 5.

82. Tompkins, "Reader in History," 203.

83. Ibid., 201.

84. Ibid., 202.

85. Jane P. Tompkins, *Sensational Designs* (New York: Oxford University Press, 1985), 60.

86. Ibid., 114.

87. Fish, *Is There a Text in This Class?* 184, 190, 193, 195.

88. Peter Lebrecht Schmidt, "Reception Theory and Classical Scholarship: A Plea for Convergence," in William M. Calder, Ulrich K. Goldsmith, and Phyllis B. Kevevan, eds., *Hypatia: Essays in Classics, Comparative Literature, and Philosophy Presented to Hazel E. Barnes on Her Seventieth Birthday* (Boulder: University of Colorado Associated Press, 1985), 67–77.

89. Hans Robert Jauss, "Sketch of a Theory and History of Aesthetic Experience," in *Aesthetic Experience and Literary Hermeneutics,* trans. Michael Shaw (Minneapolis: University of Minnesota Press, 1982), 23.

90. Ibid., 25.

91. Ibid., 23.

92. Holub, *Reception Theory,* 13.

93. S. H. Butcher, trans. and commentator, *Aristotle's Theory of Poetry and Fine Art* (New York: Dover, 1951).

94. Ibid., 121–62.

95. Ibid., 153.

96. Stephen Halliwell, trans. and commentator, *The Poetics of Aristotle* (Chapel Hill: North Carolina University Press, 1987), 71.

97. Richard Janko, trans. and commentator, *Aristotle: Poetics I* (Indianapolis, Ind.: Hackett, 1987), xv.

98. Halliwell, *Poetics of Aristotle,* 25.

99. Butcher, *Aristotle's Theory,* 207–9.

100. Ibid., 210–11.

101. Ibid., 211.

102. Ibid., 213.

103. Cleanth Brooks and Robert B. Heilman, *Understanding Drama* (New York: Holt, 1945), 485–86.

104. Tompkins, "Reader in History," 203, 207n.

Chapter 4. The Reader and the Spectators

1. Stephen Booth, "On the Value of *Hamlet,*" in Norman Rabkin, ed., *Reinterpretations of Elizabethan Drama: Selected Papers from the English Institute* (New York: Columbia University Press, 1969), 142.

2. Karen Laughlin, "'Looking for sense . . .': The Spectator's Response to Beckett's *Come and Go.*" *Modern Drama* 30 (1987), 137.

3. Ibid., 139.

4. David Scanlan, *Reading Drama* (Mountain View, Calif.: Mayfield, 1988), 170.

5. Ibid., 17.

6. Ibid.

7. Kirsten Nigro, "On Reading and Responding to (Latin American) Playtexts," *Gestos* 2 (November 1987), 108–9.

8. Laughlin, "Looking for sense," 144.

9. Nigro, "On Reading," 109.

10. Roger Gross, *Understanding Playscripts: Theory and Method* (Bowling Green, Ohio: Bowling Green University Press, 1974), 81–82.

11. Nigro, "On Reading," 111n.

12. Gross, *Understanding Playscripts,* 79.

13. Ibid., 51–52.

14. The hypothetical audience (as well as the actual and speculated audiences) serves yet another important purpose, that of allowing readers to read in a way in which they would not normally read. Jill Dolan, in her incisive study of the feminist as critic and spectator, mentions the "'resistant reader,' who analyzes a performance's meaning by reading against the grain of stereotypes and resisting the manipulation of both the performance text and the cultural text that it helps to shape"; see Jill Dolan, *The Feminist Spectator as Critic* (Ann Arbor, Mich.: UMI, 1988), 2.

Readers who are likely not to question (or, to put it in Dolan's terms, to be manipulated by) the performance and cultural texts might be able to read "against the grain of stereotypes"; likewise, readers who approach a playscript having already rejected cultural stereotypes and who are immediately conscious of the playwright's attempts to manipulate may nonetheless begin to appreciate and explore the play's impact on its original audiences.

15. Alfred Harbage, *Shakespeare's Audience* (New York: Columbia University Press, 1941).

16. Ann Jennalie Cook, *The Privileged Playgoers of Shakespeare's London, 1576–1642* (Princeton: Princeton University Press, 1981).

17. Andrew Gurr, *Playgoing in Shakespeare's London* (Cambridge: Cambridge University Press, 1987).

18. Nigro, "On Reading," 109.

19. Gross, *Understanding Playscripts*, 82.

20. Martin Esslin, *The Theatre of the Absurd*, rev. ed. (Garden City, N.Y.: Doubleday/Anchor, 1969), 1–3.

21. Stanton Garner, *The Absent Voice: Narrative Comprehension in the Theater* (Urbana: University of Illinois Press, 1989), 176n.

22. Nigro, "On Reading," 109.

Chapter 5. Playreader Audiences for Genet's *Les bonnes*

1. I will clarify some of the issues regarding the text of *Les bonnes* later in this chapter.

2. Because the immediate issue is what the writers make of the plot, I will disclose their identities after presenting their summaries.

3. All three come from press notices in response to the first production of *Les bonnes*. My reason for using these extracts (as well as the next three) is that they are far shorter and more concise than the available commentary drawn from literary criticism. I also wish to familiarize the reader with some of the drama criticism associated with this production.

However, I do not wish to be guilty of making the same leap of which I have accused Peter J. Rabinowitz and other reader-response critics—that is, of jumping abruptly from playreaders to spectators. Nor do I mean to imply here that playreaders and spectators build the same narratives. If anything, these extracts illustrate how those in the theatre audience relate more to visible action than playreaders might. Moreover, the kind of misreading evident in the second extract (about Solange playing Solange while Claire plays Madame) would be much less likely to occur for playreaders, if only because the stage directions help to identify characters' names. Nonetheless, although what spectators draw upon to construct a sense of narrative may be very different from what playreaders use, both inevitably build a "story"; in this sense all of the writers used here are "readers" of the dramatic text.

The first extract is from Robert Kemp's review of *Les bonnes* in *Le monde,* 26 avril 1947, p. 6; the second, from Gabriel Marcel's review in *Les nouvelles littéraires,* 1 mai 1947, p. 10; and the third, from J.-J. Rinieri's review in *La NEF,* 30 mai 1947, 158. (Translations for these and all subsequent reviews and for Léo Lapara's memoir are mine.)

4. Again, I offer these extracts and will identify the writers after presenting their views.

5. Again, all three come from notices in response to the first production: the first is from Thierry Maulnier's review of *Les bonnes* in *Revue de la pensée française,* août 1947, 42; the second from Hervé Lauwick's review (in *Noir et blanc;* quoted by Richard N. Coe in "Unbalanced Opinions: A Study of Jean Genet and the French Critics Followed by a Checklist of Criticism in French," *Proceedings of the Leeds Philosophical and Literary Society,* 14 [June 1970], 371); and the third, from a writer who signs his initials R.K., review of *Les bonnes* in *La gazette des lettres,* 3 mai 1947, 16; the style and tone suggest Robert Kemp, a little more thoughtful here than in his earlier review in *Le monde,* cited above.

6. J. L. Styan, *The Dramatic Experience: A Guide to the Reading of Plays* (Cambridge: Cambridge University Press, 1965), ix.

7. Jean-Paul Sartre, *Saint Genet: Actor and Martyr,* trans. Bernard Frechtman (New York: Pantheon, 1963), 611.

8. Jeannette Savona mentions the 1980 Phillip Zazzilli production of the play at Madison, Wisconsin, which "was performed by three casts simultaneously: one male, one female, and one of Buraka-like puppets . . . ." See Jeannette L. Savona, *Jean Genet* (New York: Grove, 1983), 165. Even over such multiple stagings playreaders still have an advantage. There is virtually no limit to the number of simultaneous enactments that may be "produced" in the imagination.

9. The editions of the playscript that I will use in discussing the play are the Editions Gallimard text (in French), which reflects the play as produced in 1947, and the Grove Press text (translated into English by Bernard Frechtman), which reflects the revised version first produced in 1954. The 1947 version is noticeably shorter than the play we know in English. Odette Aslan discusses at length the different versions of the text in *Jean Genet* (Paris: Seghurs, 1973), 38–43 ("L'histoire de la pièce").

I will refer to material included in both versions and will, when necessary, explain the discrepancies between them. I will also translate what is not included in Frechtman's translation. Page references will be given in parentheses rather than in notes; references for the Editions Gallimard version will be indicated by "EG" and those for the Grove Press version by "GP."

10. Savona, *Jean Genet,* 161.

11. Genet discusses his own view of the play in *Lettre à Pauvert sur les bonnes* (1954), published in English as "A Note on Theatre," *Tulane Drama Review,* 7 (Spring 1963), 37–41, and in *Comment jouer «les bonnes»* (1963), which has been published as a *notice* in the current French edition; see Jean Genet, *Comment jouer «les bonnes»* [1963], *Les bonnes* (Paris: Editions Gallimard, Collection Folio, 1976), 7–11.

12. In the French (1947) version, Solange silently faces the audience head-on, standing immobile, "her hands crossed as if manacled" (113); in the English (1954) version, Solange delivers a triumphant monologue.

13. In the 1947 version, Madame's glances and longer examinations of her-

self in the glass are not explicit, merely implied, and when Claire enters with the poisoned tea, Madame is busy looking through her armoire (EG 75). Genet seems to have further developed his use of the mirror in the 1954 version of *Les bonnes* (the French text used for the GP translation); his revisions come just two years before the first publication of *Le balcon*, in which the mirror plays an even more obvious and central role.

14. These particulars are drawn from Janet Flanner's article, "Murder in Le Mans," originally published in *Vanity Fair* and reprinted in *Paris Was Yesterday*, ed. Irving Drutman (New York: Popular Library, 1972), 98–104. Flanner, who avidly followed this trial in the daily press, recalls jokingly, "Through a typographical error the early French press reports printed the girls' name . . . as Lapin . . . ," and she later refers to the pair as "the Rabbit Sisters."

She bases her darkly humorous account on articles by the liberal Tharaud brothers in *Paris-Soir*, as did Jacques Lacan in his psychological study, "Motifs du crime paranoïaque: le crime des soeurs Papin," which was first published in the literary journal *Minotaure* in 1933 and later included in *De la psychose paranoïaque dans ses rapports avec la personnalité suivi de premiers écrits sur la paranoïa* (Paris: Editions du Seuil, 1975), 389–98.

15. Contemporary newspaper accounts of the crime itself and of the trial agree on this point. Moreover, Lacan in trying to psychoanalyze the Papins' paranoid actions, emphasizes the monstrosity of the killings in contrast to the "banal breakdown of the electric lighting," which Christine upon her arrest told authorities prompted the savageries which she and Léa perpetrated against the Lancelins (Lacan, 389).

Thus, we must be skeptical of Claude Francis and Fernande Gontier, who in their biography of Simone de Beauvoir allege that in the employers' absence the Papins

> released their frustrations in genuine psychodrama, taking turns acting out the role of the lady of the household. Caught in the act one night when the lawyer's wife and daughter returned earlier than expected, the startled servants were seized by some murderous impulse and went on a rampage.

See Claude Francis and Fernande Gontier, *Simone de Beauvoir: A Life, A Love Story*, trans. Lisa Nesselson (New York: St. Martin's, 1987), 129. Francis and Gontier credit de Beauvoir's *The Prime of Life* as the source of this information. However, although (as I make clear later in this chapter) de Beauvoir has much to say about this murder case, she never refers to the kind of role-playing her biographers attribute to the Papin sisters. The Francis-Gontier version was clearly not influenced by Paulette Houdyer's novel, *Le diable dans le peau* (Paris: R. Julliard, 1966), which does not depict the sisters engaged in playing mistress and maid. In fact, the probable source of the biographers' inventive retelling would seem to be *Les bonnes*.

16. The reader may have already perceived several problems in this assumption, which is nonetheless not an utterly unreasonable one. However, if one begins with the assumption that the playscript relies on material taken from another source, then the conclusion that the audience somehow recognized the borrowing and viewed it as meaningful, is—even if it is erroneous—perhaps inevitable. This flaw seems to run through Peter Rabinowitz's essay, discussed in chapter 3.

17. The play was published as *L'Apollon de Bellac*, and is now known under that title. I say more about this play later in this chapter.

18. Elizabeth Burns, *Theatricality: A Study of Convention in the Theatre and Social Life* (New York: Harper & Row, 1972), 181.

19. Ibid., 185.

20. Coe, "Unbalanced Opinions," 63n.

21. Ibid., 60.

22. Sartre, *Saint Genet*, 617.

23. Coe, "Unbalanced Opinions," 60.

24. Alfred Cobban, *A History of Modern France*, volume 3: *France of the Republics, 1871–1962* (Baltimore: Penguin, 1965), 210.

25. Bettina L. Knapp, *Louis Jouvet: Man of the Theatre* (New York: Columbia University Press, 1957), 224.

26. Unlike Janet Flanner, whose New Yorker pseudonym followed the traditional spelling of the French name *Genêt*, the playwright and novelist named himself without the circumflex over the second *e*. Nonetheless, early reviews of his plays often spell his name according to what was considered correct by the editorial staff.

Sartre took advantage of this confusion when he named his book *Saint-Genêt: Comédian et martyr*, which, according to Bernard Frechtman in his note on the English translation, "evokes the memory of St. Genestus (known in French as Genest or Genêt), the third-century Roman actor and martyr and the patron saint of actors." Frechtman, aware that such wordplay would seem obscure to British and American readers, named his translation of the book *Saint Genet: Actor and Martyr*. See "Translator's Note," in *Saint Genet: Actor and Martyr* by Jean-Paul Sartre, trans. Bernard Frechtman (New York: Pantheon, 1963), vii.

27. Marcel Thiebault, review of *Les bonnes*, *Carrefour* 137 (30 avril 1947), 9, and André Frank, review in *Le populaire de Paris*, 26 avril 1947, p. 2.

28. Simone de Beauvoir, *The Prime of Life*, trans. Peter Green (New York: Penguin, 1962), 131.

29. Ibid., 130–31.

30. Ibid., 132.

31. Two contributors to *Les voies de la création théâtrale IV* (which looks at various aspects of the French Garcia production) refer to the Papin sisters. Odette Aslan notes that the gestures and poses of Sylvie Belai, the actress who played Claire, seemed reminiscent of those in photos of Léa Papin; see Odette Aslan, "L'interpretation des «Bonnes»," in Denis Bablet and Jean Jacquot, eds., *Les voies de la création théâtrale IV* (Paris: Editions du Centre National de la Recherche Scientifique, 1975), 184. Aslan also reminds us that the Papins, unlike the Lemerciers, actually committed the crime, and she implies that the latter would have known about the former from *Détective* magazine, which Claire admits reading (Aslan, "L'interpretation des «Bonnes»," 196).

In her essay, Anne-Marie Gourdon, in surveying the audience, reports that only 1 percent of the spectators thought the incline of the platform in the Garcia production symbolized the staircase (on which the actual murders in Le Mans occurred). See Anne-Marie Gourdon, "«Les bonnes»: la perception de spectateur," in Denis Bablet and Jean Jacquot, eds., *Les voies de la création théâtrale IV* (Paris: Editions du Centre National de la Recherche Scientifique, 1975), 285. This is an intriguing statistic which nonetheless seems rather meaningless without other data, such as how many in the audience even knew of the Papins, etc.

32. Léo Lapara, *Dix ans avec Jouvet* (Paris: Editions France-Empire, 1975), 195.

33. Ibid., 195–96.

34. Coe, "Unbalanced Opinions," 39.

35. Rinieri, "Review in La NEF," 158.

36. Ibid., 160.

37. Maulnier, "Review," 40–42.

38. Ibid., 40.

39. Rinieri, "Review in La NEF," 157.

40. Henriette Brunot, review of *Les bonnes* in *Psyché: Revue international de psychoanalyse et des sciences de l'homme,* 8 juin 1947, 765–66.

41. Donald Inskip, *Jean Giraudoux: The Making of a Dramatist* (New York: Oxford University Press, 1958), 149.

42. Coe, "Unbalanced Opinions," 36.

43. Frank, "Review," 2.

44. Roger Lannes, review of *Les bonnes* in *Le Figaro littéraire,* 26 avril 1947, p. 6.

45. Jean Tardieu, review of *Les bonnes* in *Action: Hebdomadaire de l'indépendence française* 135, 2 mai 1947, 10.

46. Francis Ambriére, review of *Les bonnes* in *L'opéra,* 30 avril 1947, p. 1.

47. Usually commentators either do not mention the order of the pieces (such as Coe, 36, and Savona, 40), or imply that *L'Apollon* came first (such as Knapp, 226). Richard Cohen, writing on *L'Apollon de Bellac* in *Giraudoux: Three Faces of Destiny* (Chicago: University of Chicago Press, 1968), 77, is a notable exception.

Although some newspaper listings place *Les bonnes* first, others place *L'Apollon* first. Numerous reviews indicate that, contrary perhaps to present expectations, *Les bonnes* was the curtain raiser. Thus, when Lapara tells us that, after the last performance of *Les bonnes,* the curtain did not come up again, he is leaving out that it naturally had to rise once more for *L'Apollon.*

Ambriére's forty minutes may seem an extremely brief time to readers familiar with the American (1954) version of the play. Although the 1947 script is shorter than the later revision, a performance time of forty minutes suggests that the players were rushing, perhaps hoping to finish the piece as quickly as possible.

48. Coe, "Unbalanced Opinions," 39.

49. Julian Hilton, *Performance* (London: Macmillan, 1987), 128.

50. See Anne-Marie Gourdon, *Théâtre, public, perception* (Paris: Editions du Centre National de la Recherche Scientifique, 1982).

51. Daphna Ben Chaim, *Distance in the Theatre: The Aesthetics of Audience Response* (Ann Arbor, Mich.: UMI, 1984).

52. Sartre, *Saint Genet,* 611.

53. Ibid., 612.

54. The following June, Audiberti's *Le mal court* opened at the Poche, and later came premieres of such plays as Ionesco's *La Leçon* (1951), Vauthier's *Capitaine Bada* (1952), de Ghelderode's *Trois acteurs, un dram* and *Les aveugles* (1958), Vauthier's *Les prodigues* and Billetdoux's *Tchin-tchin* (1959), Obaldia's *Impromptu à loisir,* Dubillard's *Naives hirondelles,* Arabal's *Le tricycle* (1961), and Duras's *Les viaducs de la Seine-et-Oise* (1963).

Three months after Jouvet's production of *Les bonnes* had closed, the Noctambules housed Pichette's *Les epiphanies.* In 1950 the playhouse would welcome premieres of Audiberti's *L'ampélour,* de Ghelderode's *Sire Halewyn,* Vian's *L'equarissage pour tous,* Ionesco's *La cantatrice chauve,* an adaptation of Dostoyevsky's *The Possessed* (by Nicholas Bataille and Akakia Viala), and Adamov's *La grande et la petite manoeuvre.* The sources of this information are Guicharnaud and Esslin; I have also drawn from contemporary newspaper theatre listings.

For profiles of these and other small theatres in Paris during this period, see Ruby Cohn's *From Desire to Godot: Pocket Theater of Postwar Paris* (Berkeley: University of California Press, 1987).

Bibliography

Books and Articles

Adler, Mortimer J., and Charles Van Doren. *How to Read a Book.* Rev. ed. New York: Simon & Schuster, 1972.

Altschuler, Thelma, and Richard Paul Janow. *Responses To Drama: An Introduction to Plays and Movies.* Boston: Houghton Mifflin, 1967.

Anouilh, Jean. *Antigone.* In *Five Plays,* trans. Louis Galantiere, 1–53. New York: Hill & Wang, 1946.

————. *Eurydice (Legend of Lovers).* In *Five Plays,* trans. Kitty Black, 55–120. New York: Hill & Wang, 1952.

Aslan, Odette. "L'interpretation des «bonnes»." In Denis Balet and Jean Jacquot, *Les voies de la création théâtrale IV.* 173–200. Paris: Editions du Centre National de la Recherche Scientifique, 1975.

————. *Jean Genet.* Paris: Seghurs, 1973.

Beath, Robert Paul. "Towards a New Focus in Script Analysis: An Evaluation of Directorial Methods of Script Analysis Published 1960–1977." Diss., University of Utah, 1979.

de Beauvoir, Simone. *The Prime of Life.* Trans. Peter Green. New York: Penguin, 1962.

Beckerman, Bernard. *Dynamics of Drama.* New York: Knopf, 1970.

————. *Theatrical Presentation: Performer, Audience and Act.* Ed. Gloria Brim Beckerman and William Coco. New York: Routledge, 1990.

Ben Chaim, Daphna. *Distance in the Theatre: The Aesthetics of Audience Response.* Ann Arbor, Mich.: UMI, 1984.

Bennett, Susan. "The Role of the Theatre Audience: A Theory of Production and Reception." Diss., McMaster University, 1988. Subsequently revised and published as *Theatre Audiences: A Theory of Production and Reception.* New York: Routledge, 1990.

Berger, Harry, Jr. *Imaginary Audition: Shakespeare on Stage and Page.* Berkeley: University of California Press, 1989.

Blau, Herbert. *The Audience.* Baltimore: Johns Hopkins University Press, 1990.

Bleich, David. *Subjective Criticism.* Baltimore: Johns Hopkins University Press, 1978.

Booth, Stephen. "On the Value of *Hamlet.*" In Norman Rabkin, ed. *Reinterpretations of Elizabethan Drama: Selected Papers from the English Institute,* 136–76. New York: Columbia University Press, 1969.

Borges, Jorge Luis. *Labyrinths: Selected Short Stories and Other Writings.* Ed. Donald A. Yates and James E. Irby. New York: New Directions, 1964.

Brook, Peter. *The Empty Space.* New York: Atheneum, 1968.

Brooks, Cleanth, and Robert B. Heilman. *Understanding Drama.* New York: Holt, 1945.

Burns, Elizabeth. *Theatricality: A Study of Convention in the Theatre and Social Life.* New York: Harper & Row, 1972.

Butcher, S. H., trans. and commentator. *Aristotle's Theory of Poetry and Fine Art.* New York: Dover, 1951.

Campbell, Jeremy. *Grammatical Man: Information, Entropy, Language, and Life.* New York: Simon & Schuster, 1982.

Carlson, Marvin. *Theatre Semiotics: Signs of Life.* Bloomington: University of Indiana Press, 1990.

———. *Theories of the Theatre: A Historical and Critical Survey, from the Greeks to the Present.* Ithaca: Cornell University Press, 1984.

Chaudhuri, Una. "The Spectator in Drama/Drama in the Spectator." *Modern Drama,* 27 (September 1984): 281–98.

Cobban, Alfred. *A History of Modern France.* Volume 3: *France of the Republics, 1871–1962.* Baltimore: Penguin, 1965.

Cocteau, Jean. *The Infernal Machine.* In *The Infernal Machine and Other Plays by Jean Cocteau,* trans. Albert Bermel, 1–96. New York: New Directions, 1961.

———. *Orpheus.* In *The Infernal Machine and Other Plays by Jean Cocteau,* trans. John Savacool, 97–150. New York: New Directions, 1961.

———. "Preface to *Les mariés de la Tour Eiffel.*" In Toby Cole, ed. *Playwrights on Playwriting,* 240–246. New York: Hill & Wang, 1961.

Coe, Richard N. "Unbalanced Opinions: A Study of Jean Genet and the French Critics Followed by a Checklist of Criticism in French." *Proceedings of the Leeds Philosophical and Literary Society* 14 (June 1970).

Cohen, Robert. *Giraudoux: Three Faces of Destiny.* Chicago: University of Chicago Press, 1968.

Cohn, Ruby. *From Desire to Godot: Pocket Theater of Postwar Paris.* Berkeley: University of California Press, 1987.

Cook, Ann Jennalie. *The Privileged Playgoers of Shakespeare's London, 1576–1642.* Princeton: Princeton University Press, 1981.

Dolan, Jill. *The Feminist Spectator as Critic.* Ann Arbor, Mich.: UMI, 1988.

Eagleton, Terry. *Literary Theory: An Introduction.* Minneapolis: University of Minnesota Press, 1983.

Elam, Keir. *The Semiotics of Theatre and Drama.* London: Methuen, 1980.

Elliot, Susan. "Fantasy Behind Play: A Study of Emotional Responses to Harold Pinter's *The Birthday Party, The Caretaker,* and *The Homecoming.*" Diss., University of Indiana, 1973.

Else, Gerald F. *Aristotle's Poetics: The Argument.* Cambridge: Harvard University Press, 1957.

Esslin, Martin. *The Field of Drama: How the Signs of Drama Create Meaning on Stage and Screen.* New York: Methuen, 1987.

———. *The Theatre of the Absurd.* Rev. ed. Garden City, N.Y.: Doubleday Anchor, 1969.

Euripides. *Electra.* Ed. J. D. Denniston. Oxford: Clarendon, 1939.

———. *Ten Plays.* Trans. Moses Hadas. New York: Bantam, 1960.

Fish, Stanley E. *Is There a Text in This Class? The Authority of Interpretive Communities.* Cambridge: Harvard University Press, 1980.

———. *Surpris'd by Sin: The Reader in Paradise Lost.* New York: St. Martin's, 1967.

Fitzpatrick, Tim. "Playscript Analysis, Performance Analysis—Towards a Theoretical Model." *Gestos* 1 (November 1986): 13–28.

Flanner, Janet. *Paris Was Yesterday.* Ed. Irving Drutman. New York: Popular Library, 1972.

Francis, Claude, and Fernande Gontier. *Simone de Beauvoir: A Life, A Love Story.* Trans. Lisa Nesselson. New York: St. Martin's, 1987.

Frechtman, Bernard. "Translator's Note." In *Saint Genet: Actor and Martyr,* by Jean-Paul Sartre, vii. New York: Pantheon, 1963.

Freund, Elizabeth. *The Return of the Reader: Reader-Response Criticism.* New York: Methuen, 1987.

Fyfe, Hamilton, trans. *The Poetics,* by Aristotle. Loeb Classical Library. Cambridge: Harvard University Press, 1927.

Gardner, Robert. "The Dramatic Script and Procedural Knowledge: A Key to the Understanding of Dramatic Structure and a Foundation for the Development of Effective Curriculum Design in Dramatic Instruction at the Tertiary Level." Diss., University of Toronto, 1983.

Galyean, John Gilmer. "An Approach to Playscript Interpretation Based on the Poetic Theories of John Crowe Ransom." Diss., Bowling Green University, 1979.

Garner, Stanton. *The Absent Voice: Narrative Comprehension in the Theater.* Urbana: University of Illinois Press, 1989.

Genet, Jean. *The Balcony.* Trans. Bernard Frechtman. New York: Grove, 1958.

———. *The Blacks: A Clown Show.* Trans. Bernard Frechtman. New York: Grove, 1960.

———. *Les bonnes.* Paris: Editions Gallimard, Collection Folio, 1976 [1947 version].

———. *Comment jouer «Les bonnes»* [1963]." In *Les bonnes,* 7–11. Paris: Editions Gallimard, Collection Folio, 1976.

———. *Deathwatch.* In *The Maids and Deathwatch,* trans. Bernard Frechtman, 101–163. New York: Grove, 1954.

———. *The Maids.* In *The Maids and Deathwatch,* trans. Bernard Frechtman, 33–100. New York: Grove, 1954.

———. "A Note on Theatre." Trans. Bernard Frechtman. *Tulane Drama Review,* 7, 3 (Spring 1963): 37–41. [Trans. of *Lettre à Pauvert sur les bonnes.*]

———. *The Screens.* Trans. Bernard Frechtman. New York: Grove, 1962.

Giraudoux, Jean. *L'Apollon de Bellac.* Vol. 16 in *Le théâtre complet de Jean Giraudoux,* 145–196. Neuchatel: Ides et Calandes, 1951.

———. *The Apollo of Bellac.* Vol. 1 in *Four Plays,* ed. and trans. Maurice Valency, 73–101. New York: Hill & Wang, 1958.

———. *Electra.* Vol. 2 in *Three Plays,* ed. and trans. Maurice Valency, 157–247. New York: Hill & Wang, 1964.

Gourdon, Anne-Marie. "«Les bonnes»: la perception de spectateur." In Denis Bablet and Jean Jacquot, eds. *Les voies de la création théâtrale IV,* 279–90. Paris: Editions du Centre National de la Recherche Scientifique, 1975.

————. *Théâtre public, perception*. Paris: Editions du Centre National de la Recherche Scientifique, 1982.

Grebanier, Bernard. *Playwriting: How To Write for the Theater*. New York: Barnes & Noble, 1961.

Greenblatt, Stephen. *Shakespearean Negotiations: The Circulation of Social Energy in Renaissance England*. Berkeley: University of California Press, 1988.

Gross, Roger. *Understanding Playscripts: Theory and Method*. Bowling Green, Ohio: Bowling Green University Press, 1974.

Grote, David. *Script Analysis: Reading and Understanding the Playscript for Production*. Belmont, Calif.: Wadsworth, 1985.

Gruber, William. *Comic Theaters: Studies in Performance and Audience Response*. Athens: University of Georgia Press, 1986.

Guicharnaud, Jacques, and June Guicharnaud. *Modern French Theatre: From Giraudoux to Genet*. Yale Romanic Studies, 2d Series, 7; rev. ed. New Haven: Yale University Press, 1967.

Gurr, Andrew. *Playgoing in Shakespeare's London*. Cambridge: Cambridge University Press, 1987.

Halliwell, Stephen, trans. and commentator. *The Poetics of Aristotle*. Chapel Hill: University of North Carolina Press, 1987.

Harbage, Alfred. *Shakespeare's Audience*. New York: Columbia University Press, 1941.

Hayman, Ronald. *How to Read a Play*. New York: Grove, 1977.

Hilton, Julian. *Performance*. London: Macmillan, 1987.

Holden, Michael Dennis. "Literary Theory and the Education of English Teachers: An Analysis of Theories of Literature Presented in Selected Texts on Literature and Its Teaching." Diss., University of Toronto, 1973.

Holland, Norman. "Afterword." In *Shakespeare and the Triple Play: From Study to Stage to Classroom*, ed. Sidney Homan, 225–30. Lewisburg, Pa.: Bucknell University Press, 1988.

————. *5 Readers Reading*. New Haven: Yale University Press, 1975.

————. *The Dynamics of Literary Response*. New York: Norton, 1968.

————. *The First Modern Comedies: The Significance of Etheridge, Wycherley and Congreve*. Cambridge: Harvard University Press, 1959.

————. *Psychoanalysis and Shakespeare*. New York: McGraw-Hill, 1964.

————. *The Shakespearian Imagination*. Bloomington: University of Indiana Press, 1964.

Holub, Robert C. *Reception Theory: A Critical Introduction*. New York: Methuen, 1984.

Homan, Sidney. *The Audience as Actor and Character: The Modern Theatre of Beckett, Brecht, Genet, Ionesco, Pinter, Stoppard, and Williams*. Lewisburg, Pa.: Bucknell University Press, 1989.

Hornby, Richard. *Script into Performance: A Structuralist Approach*. New York: Paragon, 1977.

Houdyer, Paulette. *Le diable dans le peau*. Paris: R. Julliard, 1966.

Howes, Alan B. *Teaching Literature to Adolescents: Plays*. Glenview, Ill.: Scott Foresman, 1968.

Inskip, Donald. *Jean Giraudoux: The Making of a Dramatist*. New York: Oxford University Press, 1958.

Iser, Wolfgang. *The Act of Reading: A Theory of Aesthetic Response*. Baltimore: Johns Hopkins University Press, 1978.

———. "The Art of Failure: The Stifled Laugh in Beckett's Theater." *Bucknell Review* 26 (1981): 139–89.

Issacharoff, Michael, and Robin F. Jones, eds. *Performing Texts*. Philadelphia: University of Pennsylvania Press, 1988.

Janko, Richard, trans. and commentator. *Aristotle: Poetics I*. Indianapolis, Ind.: Hackett, 1987.

Jauss, Hans Robert. "Sketch of a Theory and History of Aesthetic Experience." In *Aesthetic Experience and Literary Hermeneutics*, trans. Michael Shaw, 3–151. Minneapolis: Minnesota University Press, 1982.

Kirby, Michael. *A Formalist Theatre*. Philadelphia: University of Pennsylvania Press, 1988.

Knapp, Bettina L. *Louis Jouvet: Man of the Theatre*. New York: Columbia University Press, 1957.

Lacan, Jacques. "Motifs du crime paranoïaque: le crime des soeurs Papin." In *De la psychose paranoïaque dans ses rapports avec la personnalité suivi de premiers écrits sur la paranoïa*, 389–98. Paris: Editions du Seuil, 1975.

Lapara, Léo. *Dix ans avec Jouvet*. Paris: Editions France-Empire, 1975.

Laughlin, Karen. "Beckett's Three Dimensions: Narration, Dialogue, and the Role of the Reader in *Play*." *Modern Drama* 28 (1985): 329–40.

———. "'Looking for sense . . .': The Spectator's Response to Beckett's *Come and Go*." *Modern Drama* 30 (1987): 137–46.

Lentricchia, Frank. *After the New Criticism*. Chicago: University of Chicago Press, 1980.

Manna, Anthony Leonard. "An Exploration of a Stage-Centered Method of Teaching Dramatic Literature with a Group of Prospective Secondary School Teachers of English." Diss., University of Iowa, 1976.

Mailloux, Stephen J. *Interpretive Conventions: The Reader in the Study of American Fiction*. Ithaca: Cornell University Press, 1982.

Mersand, Joseph. *Teaching the Drama in Secondary Schools*. Metuchen, N.J.: Scarecrow, 1969.

Nigro, Kirsten. "On Reading and Responding to (Latin American) Playtexts." *Gestos* 2 (Nov. 1987): 101–13.

Pratt, Mary Louise. "Interpretive Strategies/Strategic Interpretations: On Anglo-American Reader-Response Criticism." *Boundary 2* (Fall-Winter 1981–82): 201–31.

Quigley, Austin E. *The Modern Stage and Other Worlds*. New York: Methuen, 1985.

Rabinowitz, Peter J. *Before Reading: Narrative Conventions and the Politics of Interpretation*. Ithaca: Cornell University Press, 1987.

———. "Circumstantial Evidence: Musical Analysis and Theories of Reading." *Mosaic: A Journal for the Interdisciplinary Study of Literature* 18 (Fall 1985): 159–73.

———. "Rats Behind the Wainscotting: Politics, Convention, and Chandler's *Big Sleep*." *Texas Studies in Literature and Language* 22 (Summer 1980): 224–45.

———. "Truth in Fiction: A Reexamination of Audiences." *Critical Inquiry* 4 (Autumn 1977): 121–41.

———. "'What's Hecuba to Us?' The Audience's Experience of Literary Borrowing." In Susan Suleiman and Inge Crossman, eds., *The Reader in the Text: Essays on Audience and Interpretation*, 241–63. Princeton: Princeton University Press, 1980.

Rabkin, Norman. "Foreword." In Norman Rabkin, ed., *Reinterpretations of Elizabethan Drama: Selected Papers from the English Institute*, v–x. New York: Columbia University Press, 1969.

Reaske, Christopher Russell. *How to Analyze Drama*. New York: Monarch, 1966.

Rosenblatt, Louise M. *The Reader, the Text, the Poem: The Transactional Theory of the Literary Work*. Carbondale: Southern Illinois University Press, 1978.

Rowe, Kenneth Thorpe. *A Theater in Your Head*. New York: Funk & Wagnalls, 1960.

Sartre, Jean-Paul. *The Flies*. In *No Exit and Three Other Plays*, trans. Stuart Gilbert, 51–127. New York: Vintage, 1946.

———. *No Exit*. In *No Exit and Three Other Plays*, trans. Stuart Gilbert, 3–47. New York: Vintage, 1946.

———. *Saint Genet: Actor and Martyr*. Trans. Bernard Frechtman. New York: Pantheon, 1963.

Savona, Jeannette L. *Jean Genet*. New York: Grove, 1983.

Scanlan, David. *Reading Drama*. Mountain View, Calif.: Mayfield, 1988.

Schmidt, Peter Lebrecht. "Reception Theory and Classical Scholarship: A Plea for Convergence." In William M. Calder, Ulrich K. Goldsmith, and Phyllis B. Kevevan, eds., *Hypatia: Essays in Classics, Comparative Literature, and Philosophy Presented to Hazel E. Barnes on Her Seventieth Birthday*, 67–77. Boulder: University of Colorado Associated Press, 1985.

Scholes, Robert. *Structuralism in Literature*. New Haven: Yale University Press, 1974.

Scolnicov, Hanna, and Peter Holland, eds. *Reading Plays: Interpretation and Reception*. Cambridge: Cambridge University Press.

Stoppard, Tom. *Rosencrantz and Guildenstern Are Dead*. New York: Grove, 1967.

Styan, J. L. *The Dramatic Experience: A Guide to the Reading of Plays*. Cambridge: Cambridge University Press, 1965.

———. *The Elements of Drama*. Cambridge: Cambridge University Press, 1960.

Suleiman, Susan. "Introduction: Varieties of Audience-Oriented Criticism." In Susan Suleiman and Inge Crossman, eds., *The Reader in the Text: Essays on Audience and Interpretation*, 1980. Princeton: Princeton University Press, 1980.

Suleiman, Susan and Inge Crossman, eds. *The Reader in the Text: Essays on Audience and Interpretation*. Princeton: Princeton University Press, 1980.

Tennyson, G. B. *An Introduction to Drama*. New York: Holt, 1967.

Tompkins, Jane P. "An Introduction to Reader-Response Criticism." In Jane P. Tompkins, ed., *Reader-Response Criticism: From Formalism to Post-Structuralism*, ix–xxvi. Baltimore: Johns Hopkins University Press, 1980.

———. "The Reader in History: The Changing Shape of Literary Response." In Jane P. Tompkins, ed., *Reader-Response Criticism: From Formalism to Post-Structuralism*, 201–32. Baltimore: Johns Hopkins University Press, 1980.

——. *Sensational Designs*. New York: Oxford University Press, 1985.

Ubersfeld, Anne. *L'école du spectateur: Lire le théâtre 2*. Paris: Editions Sociales, 1982.

——. *Lire le théâtre*. Paris: Editions Sociales, 1977.

Valgamae, Mardi. "Drama as an Art Form: Four Critical Approaches." *Journal of Baltic Studies* 12 (Winter 1981): 333–39.

Vena, Gary. *How to Read and Write About Drama*. 2d ed. New York: Arco-Simon & Schuster, 1984.

Weitz, Shoshona. "Reading for the Stage: The Role of the Reader-Director." *ASSAPH: Studies in the Arts (Sec. C)* 2 (1985): 122–41.

Whitaker, Thomas R. *Fields of Play in Modern Drama*. Princeton: Princeton University Press, 1977.

Whitman, Robert F. *The Play-Reader's Handbook*. New York: Bobbs-Merrill, 1966.

Zuber-Skerritt, Ortrun, ed. *Page to Stage: Theatre as Translation*. Costerus, new series, vol. 48. Amsterdam: Rodopi, 1984.

Theatre Reviews of the 1947 Production of "Les bonnes":

Ambriére, Francis. Review in *L'opéra*, 30 avril 1947, p. 1.

Brunot, Henriette. Reivew in *Psyché: Revue international de Psychoanalyse et des Sciences de l'homme*, 8 juin 1947, 765–66.

Frank, André. Review in *Le populaire de Paris*, 26 avril 1947, p. 2.

——. Review in *Le populaire de Paris*, 6 septembre 1947, p. 2.

Kemp, Robert. Review in *Le monde*, 26 avril 1947, p. 6.

Lannes, Roger. Review in *Le Figaro littéraire*, 26 avril 1947, p. 6.

Marcel, Gabriel. Review in *Les nouvelles littiéraires*, 1 mai 1947, p. 10.

Maulnier, Thierry. Review in *Revue de la pensée française*, août 1947, p. 42.

Rinieri, J.-J. Review in *La NEF*, 30 mai 1947, 158–60.

R. K. Review in *La gazette des lettres*, 3 mai 1947, p. 16.

Tardieu, Jean. Review in *Action: Hebdomadaire de l'indépendence Française* 135, 2 mai 1947, 10.

Thiebault, Marcel. Review in *Carrefour* 137, 30 avril 1947, 9.

Index

155